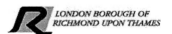

ROBINSON

First published in South Africa in 2017 by Tracey McDonald Publishers
First published in Great Britain in 2020 by Robinson

1 3 5 7 9 10 8 6 4 2

A CIP catalogue record for this book
is available from the British Library.

ISBN: 978-1-47214-468-3

Printed and bound in Great Britain by Clays Ltd, Elcograf S.p.A.

Papers used by Robinson are from well-managed
forests and other responsible sources.

MIX
Paper from
responsible sources
FSC® C104740

Robinson
An imprint of
Little, Brown Book Group
Carmelite House
50 Victoria Embankment
London EC4Y 0DZ

An Hachette UK Company
www.hachette.co.uk

www.littlebrown.co.uk

How To books are published by Robinson, an imprint of Little,
Brown Book Group. We welcome proposals from authors who
have first-hand experience of their subjects. Please set out
the aims of your book, its target market and its suggested
contents in an email to howto@littlebrown.co.uk

*I dedicate this book to my mom.*

*As a single parent, she worked two day-jobs to pay the rent, and she still waitressed at night.*

*At times we had nothing to eat, but she never stopped and that fuelled my desire never to stop – to hustle.*

# CONTENTS

# INTRODUCTION

'I wish I knew then what I know now.'

This is one of the most common laments sung by entrepreneurs everywhere. Yes, even by me and my mates. Especially by me and my mates. The lessons we've learned in the last few years have been painful, costly and, interestingly enough, common to all of us. So this book is about us trying to rectify the situation for all new business owners and aspiring entrepreneurs. We believe you can leapfrog our success by learning from our mistakes.

My first taste of business happened in Grade 6 when Harrismith Primary School held their annual entrepreneurship day. My uncle, who owned a signage shop, agreed to make me some stickers to sell. I (very innocently) committed every copyright breach in the world but soon everyone in Harrismith had my stickers on everything and I made more money in one day than I ever imagined possible. I didn't know anything about money – nor did my parents – but on this occasion I had my first experience of making my own and it ignited something in me.

The days and years that followed weren't glamorous but somehow the concept of making my own money always saved me. It allowed me to create my own wealth whilst my friends relied on their parents to give them theirs. It paid my school fees when my parents couldn't afford them.

I'm grateful for those days. They taught me many lessons and sparked within me a particular attitude: never stop trying, never stop working, never stop learning.

Entrepreneurship day was my first taste of business, and I have since become a gourmand. My life is now dedicated to entrepreneurship. I've had the greatest first-hand experiences in business – starting and selling many of them – and learned a great deal from the people I had the opportunity of working with. I've worked with thousands of small business owners (and learned a lot from each of them as well), I've funded startups and met some of the greatest tycoons. The experience of being a Shark on *Shark Tank South Africa* exposed me to even more bright-eyed ideas and disruptive models.

After all of that I'm still struck by how often failure is avoidable, and still shocked that most entrepreneurs still plunge blindly into it (90 per cent is the most accepted figure, but I think that's being generous). And they all fail because there was nobody there to steer them in the right direction. Failure is as common as the reasons for it. The difference, my friends, between a successful journey, and a wasted one, is knowing when to do what. I have seen far, far too many bright ideas fall into obscurity, dragging their authors along with them. I believe shared experience can change that.

That is what this book is about. Not science, but experience. The rules of hustle. It is an amalgamation of the epiphanies I've had, combined with those of my mentors, friends and colleagues – the giants of entrepreneurship. It's your guide to avoiding the pitfalls, as well as seizing the opportunities. It's us giving you the ability to steer yourself in the right direction. These are the rules that distinguish the successful entrepreneurs from the ones who fail: 'what to do', 'what to do sometimes' and 'what never to do'. They are also the rules that we 'successful' guys agree on, and they're the truths that I wish someone had been around to tell me when I first started on this road.

Sure, entrepreneurship is often about breaking the rules. But there are also a number of them that you should follow if you want to survive long enough to see what happens when you do.

Although I believe that both billionaire entrepreneurs and corporate workers will get something from this book, it was written mostly for the small business owner and the aspiring entrepreneur. Those who are looking for the freedom that working for oneself can bring – both financially and existentially. Those who want to create things the world hasn't yet imagined. The guys and gals who believe they can really do something great. Those who know how challenging it is to start something by yourself, and those who have no idea, but the desire to do it anyway.

I believe that anyone who has had a failed business venture will read this and identify the rules which caused them to stumble, and I hope that the entrepreneurs reading this will implement the rules and that they will make their journey easier and more enjoyable.

At twelve years old I never dreamed that this would be the life I would one day live, but today I know that entrepreneurship has the power to fix everything. I hope this book will contribute to your journey.

Starting a business should be more than just a venture – it should be an adventure!

Keep hustling!

# A LITTLE SOMETHING TO THANK YOU FOR BUYING MY BOOK

I would love to connect with you before you even start reading this book.

Please head over to www.marnusbroodryk.com/90rules and register your details.

In return you will:

1. Get 5 exclusive emails with special content reserved only for readers who registered – videos, behind the scene interviews and special deals on great products.

2. Have access to my weekly email with 5 bullet points of value to help you start, grow or manage your business. It is short and powerful and will add real value.

3. Have access to products (seminars, books, T-shirts) and events that I share exclusively with readers who register.

Let's also get social on the following platforms:

Facebook: Marnusbiz

Instagram: marnusbroodryk

Twitter: marnusbroodryk

Official hashtag: #90RulesBook

**1**

# LET'S GET A FEW
# THINGS STRAIGHT ...

As I described earlier, I believe that the reason that failure is almost a *fait accompli* for most new entrepreneurs is because they didn't really know what they were getting into. Being the engine of your own machine is very, very different from being a cog in someone else's. If you want to carve 'successful' and 'happy' on your tombstone before the word 'entrepreneur', and not the words 'failed' or 'miserable', you need to get your head straight. That is exactly what this section is about.

No matter how optimistic you are about your own business, in reality, it will not be easy. It will not be smooth-sailing. It will not be tear-free. But it may be the most exciting, liberating thing you have *ever* done – if you do it properly.

The successful journey of a self-made man (or woman, or both, or neither) is one of *contradiction*.

You see, being an entrepreneur is both entirely about *you*, as well as being not about you at all. You need to understand business, your business, and then understand that it's not all about the business. It's about keeping lean, while blossoming exponentially. Wear optimism proudly, like a top-hat, but underneath that the peaked cap of the pessimist must sit.

The successful journey is also one of *choice*:

The partners you pick – above you (investors), below you (staff) and those at your side – will either have your back, or put a knife into it. When do you hold back, and when do you leap in, with eyes shut and a prayer on your lips? When do you rely on yourself alone, and when do you actively replace yourself? You have to know when to trust, and when to play your cards so close to your chest they might as well be inside your ribcage.

Nervous? I hope so. I'm not trying to put you off, but I truly believe that more entrepreneurs would walk a wondrous path if only their first step was a little more fearful. Fear promotes caution. And caution will keep you firmly on the path, rather than set you amongst the twisted wrecks that lie, rusting, on either side.

Still excited? Brilliant. Let's get into it, shall we?

# RULE
## 1

# GET YOUR HEAD RIGHT

Dogs think like dogs, therefore they are dogs. Entrepreneurs think like entrepreneurs, therefore they are entrepreneurs. And *that's* the mindset you need. We could go on for days about what it takes to be a successful entrepreneur (and will do so, in the following pages). We could analyse the mind of an entrepreneur in a million different ways; but I'm not talking about that. I'm talking about the very first step – the mindset you need to adopt, and then embody, before you take another step. *Be* the entrepreneur before you *become* the entrepreneur.

Let's be clear: it's not for everyone … People may fly high on their corporate ladders or they may be great, talented employees, but that doesn't make them entrepreneurs. The systems are so diametrically opposed that being a 'good corporate citizen' is almost an indicator that you'll be a *bad* entrepreneur. The environment, the head-space and, yes, the rules are *not the same*.

An entrepreneur wants freedom and in return takes responsibility for everything. *Everything.* You can't ask for a pay increase, you need to hustle harder. You can't run to your senior and ask him or her to handle the difficult client, *you* need to smarten up and resolve it. No more waiting for someone to give you the right direction – you have to find it – and no referring to 'policy' to help you make a decision. No time off. No delayed responses. No sales team. The buck stops with YOU. Risks aren't always something to be avoided, but rather to be taken advantage of. The same applies to threats.

It's one hell of a mind-shift if you just came out of employment. There was always someone to go to, someone to help. Now you are on your own – naked and shivering – and you need to be OK with that. And, more importantly, you need to do whatever it takes to make it work. Hustle!

But it's not all doom and gloom. You'll probably learn more than you've ever learned in your life. You'll probably work harder than you've ever worked in your life. Fail (like most do) and you can either try again or return to the job you left and hand in your freedom for security and an orthopaedic desk chair. And if that happens, it's OK. Not everyone was born to be an entrepreneur. Some people flourish in a corporate environment and will make more money and be happier there than they'll ever be as an entrepreneur.

But pull it off and you'll be rewarded more, and be *happier* than ever before!

Still on a mission and ready to take full responsibility? Then buckle up.

---

*An entrepreneur wants freedom and in return takes responsibility for everything.*

---

# RULE
## 2

# YOU'RE NOT THE FIRST

An idea in isolation is not a business, but it may be the start of one.

If you think you've got a great, one-of-a-kind idea, I will take you a bet that it has already been thought of, or done, somewhere else in the world. And even if it hasn't, an idea means nothing if you don't do something with it. Sadly, many people have the spark of a great idea, but it fails to ignite anything. My point? The business is *not* just the idea.

The worst idea in the world executed by a pro *will be a better* business than the world's best idea executed by an amateur (if it even gets that far) ...

Xero was not the UK's first cloud accounting product. Facebook was not the world's first social network. Messrs Turner and Zuckerberg just did it *better*. They are two great examples of well-executed businesses that happened at the right time.

Those are some pretty big examples. Often you don't even *need* a great idea at all. For the entrepreneur who just wants to create a great small business, you don't have to start a revolution, but you need to spend time finding ways to improve an existing business where there is already a market. Your chances of success are higher and you'll probably find customers more quickly. Sometimes you just need to execute the existing idea *better* than the rest of your competition.

Google 'Plumber in London' and more than 56 million results appear. Think you can't open another plumbing business? Of course you can. You just need to find smarter ways of reaching your target audience, do a better job, and thus retain customers, than the other guys on the list. (In more than ten years in the property business, I still haven't found a reputable plumber.)

If you truly have a brilliant idea, execute and monetise it as fast as you can. If you want to improve an existing one, get cracking. Either way, the idea and the business which will grow from it live and die with you.

---

*The worst idea in the world executed by a pro will be a better business than the world's best idea executed by an amateur.*

---

# RULE
## 3
# REALITY RAN OUT OF CHAMPAGNE

You open Instagram and there's a video of a young guy on a yacht, girls are leaning over him and popping champagne. The video cuts to a smiling man wearing a suit and driving a Ferrari. Then text pops up: *'Live your dream, become an entrepreneur!'* Or some such horse manure.

We see inspiring quotes by Richard Branson that we should 'say YES to everything and figure it out later', over an image of him on his private island. We see images of Leonardo DiCaprio in his role as Jordan Belfort in *The Wolf of Wall Street*. Mark Cuban. Hugh Hefner.

The world has created a warped perception of entrepreneurs and their lifestyles: success, money, girls, cars, happiness, freedom. The destination is celebrated, and the journey is forgotten.

The reality is rather different. Hard work. Long hours. Failing businesses. Cash flow issues. Issues. More issues.

Few will make it. Fewer yet will make it *big*. One in ten entrepreneurs will even approach success, and maybe, *just maybe*, 1 per cent of those will see the money, girls, cars, yachts, happiness, freedom and a million followers on Instagram.

Entrepreneurs have become the rock stars of the 21st century. Everyone wants to be one. We admire the ones who made it and we don't hear much about the ones who didn't. Funnily enough, the odds of making your mark in music are slightly *higher* than the odds of a major success in business.

Don't get me wrong – entrepreneurship is amazing and I'm passionate about small businesses because I believe in them. But the world is painting a picture that is not even close to reality. If you decide to make this leap, at least know that you will give up many things in your life to chase the dream, and when things are tough you need to be willing to go to your grave still trying. At least initially, you may lose more than you gain. And when you do reap the rewards, there's a very strong chance it won't require opening up accounts in Switzerland.

If you are employed and thinking of making the move to become an entrepreneur, do it for whatever reasons you like, but never do it because you think it will be an *easier* journey, with a pot o' gold at the end. Don't do it for the champagne – you may well have to be happy with a Coke and some ice cubes. But they'll be *yours*.

---

*The world has created a warped perception of entrepreneurs and their lifestyles.*

---

# RULE
## 4

# PREPARE FOR SACRIFICE

I've worked with thousands of small business owners and the stories they tell are largely the same. They talk about how they want to spend time with their family, but they are the last to leave the office because they are working to grow their business. They pay their employees and suppliers first and hope they have enough for themselves (most days they don't). They've had to learn new skills – sometimes even new languages – and how to develop new solutions to old problems. Their sweat can be measured in buckets.

I always cringe when I hear people saying that they want to become an entrepreneur so that they can live an easier life. Or that they are working too hard in their corporate jobs and need the flexibility of entrepreneurship. The very opposite is true: entrepreneurship will take much more from you. More time, more money, more energy, more brain power. Sacrifice.

Most of your friends won't understand this journey. They work seven-hour days and warn you about burning out. They don't get why you can't drink beer with them after work or join them for the rugby match at the weekend. They gape in disbelief when you tell them you've never heard of that new TV show 'that everyone is watching'. They call you names and think you are arrogant. Your business is your everything and you live it. They don't understand and, until you actually get into it, nor will you.

Do most entrepreneurs fail because of bad business ideas? No. Lack of intelligence or knowledge? No. Underestimating the sacrifices that they needed to make in order to succeed? In most cases, absolutely. To succeed, set your expectations to their most realistic setting. Do it. Right now. Be well prepared for the fight.

I was involved in a business with a young woman who, as a result of the challenges of building her entrepreneurial dream compounded by the additional pressures of raising her children, had to sleep in her car outside the office just to get the rest she need. Elon Musk rented out his apartment, slept in the office and showered at the gym when he was starting out. But they get it: two objects cannot exist in the same space in time, and nor can your business and your family life.

The great thing? When you know what you're in for, you're prepared. When you're prepared to give it your all, you *will* do so, and you will definitely come out better at the other end. It's more rewarding than anything else. But you have to accept that along the way you'll have many late nights, you'll lose many friends and partners and you'll devote the biggest part of your life to this journey.

Be excited, just don't be fooled. You live a small portion of your life like others won't, so that you can live the rest of your life like others can't.

---

*To succeed, set your expectations to their most realistic setting.*

---

# RULE
## 5
# THE TRAP OF EMPLOYMENT

The greatest businesses nowadays were built by the youngsters of yesterday. They started from a bedroom at university. They had no debt, no expenses, no insurance; nothing to lose and everything to gain. Those lucky jerks ... Can you imagine how much easier it was for them to start from nothing, with nothing?

Not the same can be said for the mid 30-year-old with a young family, a mortgage repayment and a certain lifestyle to maintain. No matter how much this person desires to be an entrepreneur, the journey is simply not that easy. This is the story of many aspiring entrepreneurs. Something ringing true here?

Your corporate work keeps you busy most of the day and you spend whatever time you can with your family, doing chores or pursuing interests and hobbies, which means you have scant time left to start a business. And there's no way you can quit your job because you have become dependent on a monthly salary. Ironically, your desire for freedom is blocked by the necessity of security and responsibility. You are trapped by the corporate rat race. And there you will stay.

What are the options?

You could just quit, and work like flaming hell to stay afloat. This will probably require downscaling, selling your house, your car and moving in with family. To me this is dangerous, and unnecessary.

A better choice would be to smooth out the transition – to balance out your current needs with your future income – so when you do take the leap, it's more of a hop. All you really need is time, and the desire to change your life in a more comfortable fashion.

This means finding and freeing up the time you 'don't have' and dedicating it all to hustling your new business part time. Make time for it in the evenings, over weekends or in your lunch breaks. Make connections, get sales rolling. You'll essentially be working two jobs. Grow it until the transition has been sufficiently smoothed out and you can finally justify quitting your job (to yourself and to your spouse) and pursuing your dream full time.

I think we all know about these options, but they sound too difficult; too much to give up. Then be happy with where you are, because that's where you'll stay.

Unfortunately, my friend, that is what it takes to be an entrepreneur.

---

*Make time for planning your dream in the evenings, over weekends or in your lunch breaks.*

---

# RULE
## 6 GET ON WITH IT!

If you're waiting for the absolute best, no-doubt-at-all, just spot-on *perfect* time to start your business, you're going to be waiting an exceptionally long time. It will never be the perfect time. Something will always be out of whack, get in the way, throw you off. There are always better market conditions (until there aren't) and there's always just that *tiny* bit more you can save, or research, or plan ... If you wait for it, then most likely you will never start. There will always be challenges; to start the journey of an entrepreneur, you just need to take the plunge.

If you have your basic plan, you're ready. You will figure out a lot as you go along. You will see what works and what doesn't and you can adapt accordingly. Once you start serving customers, you will understand more about their needs. Once you are deep into it, you will see the real issues and problems, and there will be more of them and they will be different from what you anticipated during the planning phase.

Planning is wonderful, but not at the expense of *starting*. If you are continuously planning over a long period of time, the chances are good that your industry or customers will have changed and moved on by the time you want to go to market. Then you go into planning mode again. The cycle is repeated. Also, see RULE 2 again.

Others hear negative stories in the news and think it is a bad time to start a business. It's *always* a bad time to start a business for one reason or another. And if, hypothetically, it was an amazing time to start a business, most of those who started at the top of the wave wouldn't survive the stormier times. A good business and, more importantly, a good entrepreneur, will still get it right.

Stop making excuses, stop planning, stop deferring and just start. Now is the best time ever. If you feel strongly about it, make it happen. Now. If you don't you will always look back at this day and wish you had made the decision earlier. Regret feels far worse than failure.

*Planning is wonderful, but not at the expense of starting.*

# RULE
## 7

# MAKE THE JUMP

## BY DIVAN BOTHA

*I met Divan on the kykNET show Winslyn, which he hosts and for which I do an SME segment. We found we had a lot in common, and he became a client at The Beancounter and a business friend. Apart from his TV show prowess, he is an entrepreneur in the hospitality space, having started The Whippet Coffee in Linden and Flight Coffee, which trains championship-level baristas to make ethical coffee.*

The greatest entrepreneurs are often caught up in, and locked down by, the corporates for whom they work, where entrepreneurship is seen, by default, as a last resort. Failure is frowned upon rather than admired, so even families still discourage their members from taking the plunge because, to their minds, the risks outweigh the rewards. What will you do if it doesn't work? How will you pay the rent? And you'll be told that going on your own is a total waste of all the time you spent studying – rather just find a 'real' job. So, society at large isn't exactly encouraging you to 'make the jump'.

But isn't that a greater reason to do so? Doesn't that amp up the thrill? Yes! You're doing something that everyone else is too scared to contemplate and thus you are leaving them far behind. That's what makes entrepreneurship so invigorating, and the jump is just the beginning.

There will never be a perfect moment to jump – it does not exist. The journey is not perfect, neither the start, nor the process, nor the end. But making the jump is the only way to set out on the path less travelled.

Any of you who have bungee jumped will know what I'm talking about. You step up, walk *right* to the edge, and look down. The fear is as daunting as it is defining – it's the whole point! All the advice about what to do before you hurtle into the void is pretty much useless – it comes down to the relationship between you and your fear. Because it's that fear – of missing out, of letting yourself down, of *regret* – that will be the reason you inevitably take a deep breath, bend your knees and LEAP. And afterwards? You'll have a story you'll be telling for weeks on end, and an experience few others will even understand.

So don't listen. Ignore the rest because they don't get it. Just jump!

# RULE
## 8

# HAVE A MINDSET FOR CHANGE

Ancient Greek philosopher Heraclitus famously said that 'change is the only constant in life'. It's become somewhat trite, but is no less true. Different versions and expansions of this concept are taught at every seminar, written in every book, and PowerPointed by executives and guest speakers at every conference from here to Hong Kong. But we *still* reject it. We *get* it, but we don't *accept* it. We resist change. It's uncomfortable. We want things to stay the way we know and we fight to keep it that way.

As entrepreneurs, we need to get rid of the mindset that is resistant to change – more than *any*one else, no matter how hard it may be. We need to learn to embrace change; love it, even, to stitch it into the fabric of our jackets. Because, if we don't, we die. If you look back in history, it's not difficult to understand how dramatically things can change in a short period of time.

In the 1970s nurses sold cigarettes in hospital wards (I'm not kidding). Patients bought them and smoked them in their beds. Cigarette brands produced TV ads using doctors for testimonials, claiming that their cigarettes reduced stress and that 'most doctors smoke Camel cigarettes'. It's almost unbelievable. Yet in the 1970s – just 40 years ago – it was reality. How different things are now, and how *weird* is that past? Now apply this forward. In 2050, people will look back at 2020 and laugh at the things we are doing now. That is change, and change is life.

Entrepreneurs who find a way to embrace the mindset of constant change, knowing that things will never be the same, are the ones who are able to create great, sustainable businesses. Not necessarily by predicting the future, but by accepting the fact that it won't look like today – and being ready for it.

History books are full of entrepreneurs and businesses who stuck to their guns and were soon out on the street. The most often quoted examples are Nokia, BlackBerry, Kodak and Blockbusters, but there are thousands of others you'll probably never hear of. Conversely, some of the biggest companies that are still around today are almost unrecognisable from what they once were. Remember, Netflix started as a DVD rental business, and IBM now specialises in consulting and IT services.

Change is like a roller coaster. The big machine will move whether you like it or not. You can be the idiot who tries to hold it back and gets crushed to death, or you can jump on and have one hell of a ride.

When it comes to change, resistance is absolutely futile. Entrepreneurs – *successful* entrepreneurs – don't even bother trying.

---

*Accept the fact that the future won't look like today – and be ready for it.*

---

# RULE
## 9 THOUGHTS BECOME THINGS

Perhaps in the next 50 years we will discover the true power of our subconscious mind but, for now, I don't know how much I go in for all the theories around positive thinking, visualisation and new age religions ... But, what I do know is that, for whatever reason you like, we can literally change our immediate reality by changing our thoughts. Whatever we think, we experience. Reality itself is subjective, and those who thrive and those who barely survive are separated by a conscious decision to see the world in a particular way.

Stop reading, close your eyes, and think about the colour red. Then open them again and look around. Do you notice how red is suddenly popping up everywhere? You will see the smallest red spot because you are thinking about the colour. Now do the same, but think about a nice, ocean blue. Suddenly red is no longer relevant; blue is all you see. The same thing happens when you hear a word you have never heard before; inexplicably you will hear it ten times the following week. You buy a new car, one you've never seen before on the road; suddenly everyone is driving that particular car. These are simple examples, but they demonstrate how our minds work.

Did the world change? Were there more red or blue colours? Was the word actually mentioned more? Did everyone check your Instagram and decide, suddenly, to buy that car? No, your thoughts changed, and that changed your experience of reality.

And it is no different in business. When entrepreneurs look at challenges as opportunities that is what they will see and experience. They will see a chance for success where others are seeing only the negatives. When the country is downgraded to junk status, or the economy is stagnating at 0 per cent growth, entrepreneurs with the right mindset will see those opportunities for what they are and will thrive when others are going bust.

You can't control many things, but you can control your own thoughts. And thoughts will become things. As an entrepreneur, how you *decide* to see the world will dictate how you experience it and, therefore, whether or not you succeed in it.

---

*When your thoughts change, so does your experience of reality.*

---

# RULE 10

# THE ONLY CERTAINTY IN LIFE IS DEATH

We don't know much about tomorrow. We don't know much about anything, really. But the one thing we do know for certain is that we will all die. We just don't know when. But we live as though we are immortal beings, believing that death will never happen to us, and there's still infinite time to fix things, or to 'make things right'. So, we live unethical lives, trying to screw everyone. Then unexpectedly we become sick and lie on our deathbed regretting a poorly lived life. I've seen it happen.

But it goes much, much further than that. As entrepreneurs and small business owners, we have the power and the responsibility to change the world for the better. We can serve through our products and services. We can employ people, and we can make dreams come true. It is an opportunity many aren't given, and even fewer make use of.

Many businesses are started as a rejection of something someone felt was *wrong*. Someone wanted to make a difference. But not long into the journey, they have become the companies they so desperately hated and never wanted to be like. Don't be this 'someone'.

Death is the great equaliser. When it happens, you will lose everything you have right now. Yes, everything. And not just material stuff either. You will lose your husband, your wife.

You will lose your children, your parents. You will lose the house you have just bought. And you will be lost to all of them.

The way we build businesses, and our outlook on entrepreneurship, would change drastically if we remained conscious of the fact that it will all end, and all that will be left is a legacy and an epitaph. What that epitaph says, and the number of people who will read it, is up to us. Since we will lose all our money when we die there is no sense in accumulating it in the questionable way we do.

Now, please think about this, and then think about what you really want to do right here and now, and the type of business you want to create: the legacy you want to leave. Start working on it today. If you had just 21 days left on planet earth, what would you do with them? Don't let regret be the last feeling you have. All that will remain of you are the ripples you made across the world while you were here, so make them *good* ones.

---

*Don't let regret be the last feeling you have.*

---

# RULE
## 11

# DON'T GO BROKE TRYING TO LOOK RICH

Some very insightful person once said, 'Entrepreneurship is living a few years of your life like most people won't, so that you can spend the rest of your life like most people can't.' I like to repeat it because it's *that* relevant a reminder.

The time referred to is what you need to put in to make things work, and the sacrifices you will need to make, but it is equally true when considering your own personal expenses and lifestyle.

People often exit corporate life and start their own businesses thinking they can maintain their lavish lifestyles. In rare cases this can be done but, in most cases, it just isn't possible. A new business will take a lot from you and initially that might also mean all the cash available. Cut back on your own lifestyle to get your business off the ground.

There is nothing worse for a new entrepreneur than to be continuously running out of funds because of unnecessary personal expenses. Growing and funding the business is already hard enough; there is definitely no space to fund you as well. You need to ask yourself a question: 'Do I spend like I'm already a millionaire, or do I dedicate all my focus and resources into ensuring I become a millionaire?'

New entrepreneurs are often under pressure to 'show off'. You started your own business and now you want to show the world how successful you are to justify your initial decision. To prove to your old boss that you've made it, to convince your friends that the missed beers and birthdays paid off. So you buy fancy cars, new laptops every month and slick suits and commit to other unnecessary personal expenses. And before you know it, you've outspent yourself. If you have investors in your business, you will soon piss them off because all the business's cash flow goes into funding your own Rich and Famous Lifestyle. And when the business finally runs out of cash, you will find it impossible to convince them to give you any more. It's a slippery slope, all the way down to Broketown.

Taken all round, it is just bad business, but it is even worse for the entrepreneur still trying to make it. So don't fall for this. Rather take a back seat, see how you can scale down on personal expenses and put all your efforts and cash into the business. Don't live off finance and loans – it is expensive. Live just *behind* your means. Cut back, get things going and once you have it all worked out you will have an amazing life with excess cash that you can spend on the good things in life.

Then. Not now.

---

*Would you rather act like a millionaire, or be one?*

---

# 2

# ENTREPRENEURIAL BUSINESS STAGES

Despite what you've been told, there aren't a lot of rules that will apply to all parts of your journey. There are even fewer 'silver bullets' (although the second half of this book is riddled with them). What was critical yesterday won't be worth spit tomorrow, and that's your life.

This section of the book is designed to show you what to expect, and hopefully what to *do*, at the different phases of your entrepreneurial life. It's all about taking the right step at the right time.

# THE RIGHT STEP AT THE RIGHT TIME

## Part 1: The early years

There are different phases to building a business – obviously. What may not be so obvious are the rules that apply at different stages, and how those rules change as you progress. You've heard the expression 'what got you here won't get you there' and it's true. Mostly. How you begin your new business – the formative years – is crucial to setting up the following ones. Keep lean, keep planning, and keep hustling.

# RULE
## 12

# THE ONE-PAGE DYNAMIC PLAN

The logic behind a business plan is great. It's a plotted journey, with marked goals and targets. It gives you something to work on, and work towards. And you'll definitely need one if you're looking for financing. But very seldom does it actually become a real working document for the small business owner; business plans are too long-winded and rigid and don't allow for the fast changes and flexibility you're going to need when you start up. So, gut instinct is how most survive, and the plan goes into the middle drawer.

That doesn't mean you don't need a plan. It just means you need a different kind of plan – one that works for you at the stage you're at. A one-pager plan that acts as a *dynamic* working document is where it's at. The key word here is *dynamic*.

Try to compile a one-pager of what you aim to achieve in the next year. Break it down per month and list the small steps that you will be taking to reach your bigger vision at the end of the year. This plan could include anything, but you should know that it will be your guide to what is important and what isn't.

Work on it weekly, review it monthly and ensure that you are moving in the right direction. At the start of every month, review your plan and list your priorities for the month. If you hit a snag, stop, re-evaluate your plan, make changes and move on. It is not set in concrete. It is *dynamic*.

Too many entrepreneurs go to work each day and solve issues as they arise without planning proactively for what they want. Others view their business plan – all 100 pages of it – like it's the Bible. Neither approach will get you very far.

The one-pager will be your plan, your guide. Keep it with you all the time so it can be as flexible as you need to be.

---

*Re-evaluate your plan, make changes and move on.*

---

# RULE
## 13

# KNOW YOUR BREAK-EVEN FIGURE

In a very complicated world, it is always great to simplify things – to have goals, a clear vision, a one-pager plan. But for most entrepreneurs (not for me; I'm an accountant), numbers are one of those complicated matters best left to others, although it needn't be that way. And when it comes to one particular number, it *cannot* be that way: that number is the break-even figure. It's the one number every entrepreneur must know. If you don't have a break-even figure, how will you know if you're succeeding or failing?

A break-even figure is the amount of sales you need to make in a month to cover all expenses and to make a target profit. If you can calculate this, then you have a number that you can chase every day – something that is measurable and understandable for the entrepreneur.

The break-even figure is calculated by using three figures:

1. *Gross Profit Percentage*: Your gross profit percentage is calculated by taking your gross profit (sales minus cost of sales) divided by your sales. Let's say you sell a product for £20 and the cost of that product is £15, then your gross profit will be £5. Your gross profit percentage therefore is 20 per cent (sales (£20) divided by gross profit (£5)).

2. *Overheads*: Overheads are the total of all your fixed expenses each month. Examples include rent, salaries, Internet, fuel and all other costs that you need to pay, e.g. £2,000.

3. *Profit Target*: This is the profit you would like to achieve in a month, e.g. £10,000.

Now that we have these three figures, we can calculate our break-even amount:

Break-even = (overheads + profit target) *divided by* gross profit percentage

So, continuing the example:

Break-even = (£2,000 + £10,000) / 20% = £60,000

This means that you must make sales of £60,000 per month to cover all your overheads and achieve your profit target.

If you have this figure you can now plan how to achieve this target and go out every day chasing a goal, rather than just crossing your fingers ... One can take this number and divide it by the number of working days in a month to get to a daily target of sales.

Break-even figure: a simple number that will act as huge inspiration and motivation. Make sure it's on your one-page dynamic plan.

---

*A break-even figure is the amount of sales you need to make in a month to cover all expenses and to make a target profit.*

---

# RULE 14

# USE WHAT YOU'VE GOT

There are really just two ways to start a business: you either draw up a business plan and go and look for funding, or you just start with what you have and you hustle your way to the top. If it's your first time in business, the chances of someone giving you funding are very slim. (Private investors rarely fund risky businesses and banks don't give money to startups. Why not? Because banks are in it to make money and you won't be doing that. The chances of you messing up are a whole lot greater.) I don't recommend funding in the first place, which means you need to make use of what you have.

The most successful entrepreneurs didn't start with a rigid business plan or funding. Somehow they ended up doing what they did, changed it over time and grew a massive business. You can, and should, do the same.

Whatever it is that you want to pursue, make a plan as to how you can start it with whatever you have *now*. Maybe you want to set up a restaurant? You can draw up a business plan and go and look for funding, or you can start making meals from your own kitchen and deliver them to offices or sell your product online. The former is unlikely to succeed, and the latter is less risky. Seems like a no-brainer to me. Using what resources you already have will save you millions in set-up costs and thousands in monthly overheads. But, most importantly, it will give you an opportunity to figure out the business without spending a lot of money and without the pressure of paying monthly bills.

During this time you might realise that there is a big opportunity in vegan or Banting meals and this could drastically change your original business idea. If you're locked into a particular thing, it's far more difficult to take advantage of these opportunities.

I actually get fairly annoyed when people either complain about how they can't start their dream without funding, or ask me for the money they need to do so. If a small-town boy from Harrismith could start a business with £2,000 in savings and a rented pick-up truck, and still manage to sell that business for millions, so can everyone else. Hustle!

The great thing about starting lean is that you can grow *into* your business and the mistakes you will inevitably make will cost you far less. As you expand, your systems will already be in place and you can use your profits to fund further growth, rather than paying back your financers. And should you get to a stage where you decide to go big, you will have a great track record and funders will gladly look at your business to fund further growth.

---

*Using what you already have will save you millions in set-up costs and thousands in monthly overheads.*

---

# RULE
## 15

# OVER-PREPARE TO UNDER-SUCCEED

Mistakes happen. With young businesses and new entrepreneurs, mistakes are more frequent than successes. Welcome to reality. I've yet to see a business plan that met the targets the entrepreneurs believed it could 'conservatively' achieve. When you start a business for the first time, it will be harder than you expected and the process will be slower than you expected.

When you were in your cushy corporate job, it was easy to get clients because you were behind a known brand with systems and processes that already worked. Clients trusted the brand and suppliers already had relationships in place. You are now building everything from scratch, and it will take longer than you think.

Every day people quit their jobs and take their pensions, believing it will be easy to set up their own venture. It won't be. Customers will promise to support you when you start your own business, and then they are slow to move over. Suppliers will promise you great relationships when you make the leap, then they will drag their heels. Be prepared for all of the above.

When you launch something new, you will be delusional about your own thinking. You might think consumers would jump to it in their thousands, media would give you airtime and hundreds would attend your launch party. I'm sorry, they won't. So, be prepared for it.

Your new business or product will take time to get out there. Every day will be like climbing a mountain. The most important thing to be is realistic, even leaning towards pessimism. Expect things to be worse than you imagined and be prepared. Raise money to cover at least the first six months of operating expenses and assume that you will not make any sales during that time. If you do, see it as a bonus and a buffer for the next six months.

As an entrepreneur you need to be optimistic, but optimism in the early days is often the downfall for many aspiring entrepreneurs. A little bit of pragmatism will go a long way to making sure your business takes off.

*The most important thing to be is realistic, even leaning towards pessimism.*

# RULE 16 WALK BEHIND YOUR SUCCESS

Don't start big. And don't try to get there before your time. If it is the first time you have ventured into the entrepreneurial space, don't start with big commitments. Don't hire big offices or retail spaces. Don't employ expensive staff. Don't overextend yourself. It is great to *think* big, but you need time to action your big plans.

Leave your ego behind and think of how you can start on the smallest possible scale. It is easy and great to learn and make mistakes when you are small. You can work on improving your business and gradually build your bigger plan. Walk *behind* your success. Trust me, it's the safest place to be.

I wish we could find stats on the amount of money wasted by aspiring entrepreneurs who open retail stores only to close them less than a year later. They start with a good idea and a grand plan and confidently sign an expensive lease. Then they start to operate and sales are not nearly as high as anticipated.

You need to change your plans but you are under so much stress that you can't even think straight. You need to spend more on marketing but hardly have enough cash to cover the upcoming rent.

There is a better way: start small, work from home or co-rent a space, or sell online. Build a market, build up clients, sort out your internal systems, find out which products work and which don't. Once you have got it right, come up with a bigger plan. Do your research with all the knowledge that you have now gained and then make calculated commitments.

Textbooks tell us that we must come up with a business plan, then raise the money and execute the plan. Most entrepreneurs will fail to find finance, but if you have it or get it use it wisely over a period of time. This is a marathon, not a sprint. Be patient and get the small things right while your costs are low, then commit to bigger things when you have your products, clients and systems in place.

---

*This is a marathon, not a sprint.*

---

# RULE
## 17 SHORT CUT SUICIDE

Starting a business is risky enough without adding other unnecessary risks. Put simply, don't get involved in anything illegal, don't do anything that is ethically questionable and always pay your debts. Don't take short cuts.

At the start it might be appealing to get caught up in the next big thing, but it's often 'big' because there is something dodgy about it. Be careful. Getting business by paying bribes or becoming the next tenderpreneur might be momentarily lucrative, but never pays off in the long run. Do you want to be a thief or an entrepreneur? Steal money, or create wealth? It may be morally arguable to use pirated software or tweak your profits so you keep more for yourself; after all, isn't that how all small businesses do it? By taking short cuts? No, it isn't. And you're getting yourself entangled in a net you may not be able to get out of one day …

And it goes further than that. Be ethical in the day-to-day running of your business. Pay your taxes. Structure your tax affairs so that you pay the minimum that you legally can, but don't try to bullshit anyone. (I had a friend who always said that if you think your taxes are too high, then you are not making enough money. Rise above it.) The truth *will* out, and you'll be left with the consequences.

You're probably not a bad person, and you can justify the morally grey moves you make. Initially it may feel bad, but over time it will become your norm and then, yes, you *are* a bad person. The decisions you make in the early days are the foundations upon which the rest of your business is built. All shaky foundations usually come crumbling down in the end.

I can't think of anything more depressing than working on your business for five to ten years just to lose everything because of stupid decisions you made early on. There are a thousand examples of how you can get caught running a dishonest operation. I've seen many people lose their businesses because of a tax audit; some even literally ended their own lives. It's just not worth it. Remember: what goes around comes around.

---

*The truth will out, and you'll be left with the consequences.*

---

# RULE
## 18

# THE RIGHT CORPORATE STRUCTURE

When you start your business, there are different structures you can set up in which to operate. Most commonly, you can either register a company, or trade in your personal name. Pick the one that makes the most sense for you – there is no 'right' answer.

Registering a company essentially creates a separate entity, and offers many benefits. The most important ones are:

- *Tax Benefits*: There are numerous tax benefits if you register as a company. You can also structure your tax affairs better and pay less tax.

- *Reputation*: Customers, especially those you've never worked with before, need reassurance that you are a legitimate business. A potential client may suspect your business of being a 'fly-by-night' operation if your company isn't properly registered.

- *Less Risk*: Because a company is seen as a separate entity, it means that you (as the owner) are much less at risk if something goes wrong than when you are dealing under your own name.

The downside of registering a company is that you need to comply with more rules and regulations and it can be a costly exercise. So, what do you do? If you are serious about your business, then register a company and do it properly.

There will be a cost but it should be outweighed by the tax benefits, reputational clout and the legal protection it offers.

However, if you are in a position where you want to first see whether or not the business will work out, do it in your personal name. You can then register a company once your business has proved to be successful. Nine out of ten companies that are registered never trade. What a waste of time and money!

Whatever you decide, make sure it fits your business and the plans you have for it.

---

*Make sure you have the right corporate structure for your business and the plans you have for it.*

---

# RULE
## 19

# THE TECHNICAL PERSON DILEMMA

A large number of people who start businesses are technical people. Initially, they work for someone and do most of the work, until they get to the point where they ask: 'Why should I do all the work and get paid 10 per cent of what the company earns? I'm doing all the work anyway.' One day they resign and open up their own shop. Does this sound like something you may do?

In the beginning everything is amazing; you work half the time and earn double the money. But a series of business problems sets in – marketing, sales, processes, ordering, billing, invoicing and chasing outstanding money. At your previous job, someone *else* did all of that. Now it's you, and you alone. Soon you spend more time running the business than actually servicing customers. And you hate it, you are a 'technical person' and would rather cut out your eyes than deal with all the admin.

So you decide to hire someone to do the technical work while you run the business. They are not half as good as you, so you fire them and hire someone to do the admin. Things are back on track but soon you also need to manage that person as well as manage customers. The wheels come off.

On the flipside, you sometimes have business-minded entrepreneurs who don't have a clue about the technical aspects. Luckily for them, it is easier to be an entrepreneur and hire a technical person, than being a technical person who needs to find an entrepreneur to run and grow the business.

The big lesson: being a great technical person won't make you a great entrepreneur. One should never confuse the two.

Because of this, most successful businesses are built by two partners: one is the entrepreneur, the other is the technical person. The product may be crucial, but without the business to sell it and support it, it's useless. If you are the technical person, find the right partner, or be prepared to do everything yourself.

> *The big lesson: being a great technical person won't make you a great entrepreneur. One should never confuse the two.*

# RULE
## 20
# (PAYING) CUSTOMERS FIRST!

Without customers your business is nothing. Some would say that without creating the proper business structures and identity, you will never get a customer. Bit of a chicken/ egg thing happening here? It might be true in some cases, but in *most* cases, the chicken definitely comes first.

Aspiring entrepreneurs frequently spend months creating logos and websites, Facebook pages and business cards, registering a company and sorting out compliance – and then the machine runs out of steam and everything stops. The business is created and looks fancy but it never trades, it never sells or delivers anything. It never makes a cent. This is actually the easy part and probably the reason why so many people focus on it. The important part is *finding your first paying customer*.

Nobody wants to be first through the door. The first customer will probably be the hardest one to find. But once you have one, it's far easier to get two. Then four. And so on. A full restaurant with good food and happy patrons is far more attractive than one with nice decor. Focus on getting the customers!

Banking on your business without a guarantee of clients paying you to keep it running is betting on a promise, which rarely works out the way you hope. We opened a branch of The Beancounter based on the promises of potential clients who were 'absolutely going to join you as soon as the office is up'. They didn't, and we had a few rocky months. My ex-hair stylist did the same; he opened his own salon on the basis of his clients' promises that they'd 'absolutely, positively get our hair done with you'. They didn't, and eventually he had to go back to his old job. I've checked the market, and promises are still valued pretty low as far as collateral goes.

The kind of customer you need to find is a *paying* one. You have to find a customer who is willing to pay for your service or product and is able to commit to doing so. I said, COMMIT to it by PAYING for it. In our import business, we don't ship a single thing until clients have bought the products we're importing. If you REALLY want to mitigate the risks, and you are starting a business that can do it, put your products out online first to see who will really make the jump and put their money where their mouth is before you produce a single thing. Test the waters.

Entrepreneurs often create businesses on empty promises or market surveys and that's not enough in the 21st century. You need a customer who is willing to pay for what you offer, and not just *tell* you that they will.  Once you get that right, the rest becomes dramatically easier.

---

*The kind of customer you need to find is a paying one.*

---

# RULE 21 UNDERSTAND THE NUMBERS

Not all entrepreneurs are financial people. In fact, very *few* entrepreneurs are financial people. I'm not saying you should find an accountant on day one (actually, I would recommend that you don't find an accountant until you have a proper business going, but more on that later) but you need to understand the basic mechanics of business in general and, more importantly, *your* business.

And basic numbers boil down to two things when you start off: profit and cash flow.

- *Profit*: How much money will you have left after you have covered your costs and your taxes? It is important to understand both of these intimately, as well as anything else that might play a role, so that you can determine the right selling prices. Entrepreneurs often start a business, throw all their resources and savings into it, only to get unexpected bills at the end of the day that eat away all the profit or, in most cases, make them run at a complete loss.

- *Cash flow*: Cash flow is a metric of exactly how much money is running into, and out of, your business. A great profitable business might still run into serious cash flow issues. Profit does not always mean cash flow. You can invoice large amounts of money but if you don't receive the cash, you will find yourself in deep trouble (see the next rule). Or you might need to carry a large amount of stock and pay your suppliers immediately while it takes ages for your customers to pay you.

To overcome these issues simply draft a budget that ensures that you understand all your costs and that you can ask the right price for your product/service. Then look at the timing of paying and receiving these amounts and ensure that you will have enough cash available to make the payments. Once you have this prepared, run it past someone who understands, and get their input.

Entrepreneurs are often so excited about starting their new business that they forget about the only thing that counts when it comes to making money – numbers.

---

*You need to understand the basic mechanics of business.*

---

# RULE
## 22

# YOU ARE NOT A BANK

Say this with me: 'I am NOT a bank.' Say that to yourself every day. Cars run on petrol. Bodies run on oxygen. Businesses run on *cash flow*. Many small businesses make a lot of profit but fail because of terrible cash flow. As a new entrepreneur this can be confounding. On paper, you are enjoying a great profit, but you have no money.

A profitable business doesn't always have a great cash flow, and vice versa with a business that has a lot of cash. Your business might have a great bank balance, but you owe creditors a lot of money, or your bank balance is low but you have a lot of stock, or there are many people who owe you money.

Cash is king for all businesses. For entrepreneurial businesses, cash is god.

The most common, and avoidable, reason that businesses starve without cash is simply because their customers are not paying them. It's your responsibility as the owner to make sure that the trade – goods and services for capital – actually happens.

It is critically important that you put a good credit system in place so that you know on a daily or weekly basis exactly who owes you money and when they are going to pay you. With today's technology, it is possible to automatically remind your clients to pay their bill by sending them a text message or email. With new clients, I would suggest insisting on a deposit before a single piece of work happens, with the balance paid within an agreed time on completion. When customers' accounts fall into arrears, it is important to take action as soon as possible. Young businesses often don't want to annoy late-paying clients by nagging them and leave overdue clients until the last minute – and then it is usually too late to save anything.

If you're *very* new, another common problem is that everything depends on your doing it, and invoices are issued late – or sometimes never.

Only one out of ten new businesses survive the first year, and most businesses struggle to cope thereafter because of cash flow problems. Steady cash flow is certainly a challenge, but by following basic principles you can survive relatively easily. Most entrepreneurs realise this too late and then it is very difficult to change things. Make sure you start today and realise that cash is indeed king!

It doesn't matter how much money you have on paper. What matters is how much you have in the bank. You can't run a business on promises. Ask anyone who's ever tried.

---

*Cash is king for all businesses. For entrepreneurial businesses, cash is god.*

---

# RULE
## 23

# CHANGE YOUR MINDSET

### BY FARREN MARÉ

*We tried to hire Farren as a product manager at The Beancounter. His company decided to promote him, rather than lose him, so it never happened. But I was so impressed that I made him a partner. He is now the brains behind our tech division, and has enabled us to do many cool things in the tech space (see RULE 19). Moving from thriving in a corporate business to thriving in an entrepreneurial one gives him an insight into the differences between the two. I have learned so much from Farren, and I believe you will too.*

The following stems from the mindset an individual will carry as he traverses the plethora of working environments and, in particular, the conscious mind-shift one needs to make when moving from a corporate environment to the wonderful, entrepreneurial world of startups and SMEs.

Rather than accepting how things are, you need to question everything in an effort to continuously improve on what has been implemented in the past. A famous social experiment was conducted that I believe explains how people think, and how entrepreneurs should *not* behave:

A group of scientists placed five monkeys in a cage, and in the middle they placed a ladder with bananas on the top. Every time a monkey went up the ladder, the scientists soaked the rest of the monkeys with cold water. After a while, every time a monkey started up the ladder, the others would pull it down and beat it up. After a time, no monkey would dare to try to climb the ladder, no matter how great the temptation.

The scientists decided to replace one of the monkeys. The first thing the new monkey did was start to climb the ladder. Immediately, the others pulled him down and beat him up. After several beatings, the new monkey learned never to go up the ladder, even though there was no evident reason not to, aside from the beatings. A second monkey was replaced and the same thing happened. The first monkey participated in the beating of the second monkey. A third monkey was replaced, with the same result. The fourth monkey was replaced, again producing the same result, before the fifth monkey was finally replaced as well.

What was left was a group of five monkeys which – without ever having received a cold shower – continued to beat up any monkey who attempted to climb the ladder.

If it was possible to ask the monkeys why they had beaten up those who attempted to climb the ladder, their most likely answer would have been: 'I don't know. It's just how things are done around here.'

In the corporate world, many of us do things as they have always been done. It's difficult to change these processes and the mindsets behind them. When moving to the SME space you have the opportunity and responsibility to constantly ask yourself if what you're doing today will help you achieve your end goal of tomorrow and, more importantly, you need to go back and make sure your solution is still relevant on an ongoing basis. This can be a great tool for personal growth as well.

---

*Constantly ask yourself if what you're doing today will help you achieve your end goal of tomorrow.*

---

# THE RIGHT STEP AT THE RIGHT TIME

## Part 2: Up and sprinting

So you've made it this far? Well done! You can now count yourself among just a small percentage of entrepreneurs who did so. But things are getting serious. It's time to look at what's working, find out what could work better, and start leaving your bad habits behind. It's time to do more, and to do it better, and to do both of those even faster.

# RULE
## 24
# OUTBUILD YOUR COMPETITION

A report by World Wide Worx looked at the state of small businesses and found that competition was an entrepreneur's greatest challenge when it came to starting a new business.

Why do we see competition as such a big challenge and how can we overcome it?

Obviously, you need to find out who your competition is and what they do, what they offer and what their unique selling proposition is so that you can work out how to differentiate yourself from them. Know thy enemy.

But don't get obsessive about your competition. If you're always looking over your shoulder, you're not looking forward. And if you're keeping both eyes on them, who's watching your own business? Competitors should be noted, but it is more important to focus on what *you* do and to come up with new ideas and products. Outbuild them, rather than try to keep pace with them.

Many entrepreneurs feel that they must focus on price and that their products or services must be as cheap as possible, but times have changed and many customers look at the service they receive as a distinguishing factor, rather than price alone. The point is that you need to offer something unique to the market and you will succeed if you can give better service than anyone else, even if your competition is cheaper.

We live in a time where there is a lot of information available and increasing competition, but by doing some basic things right, you can keep your competition under control and you can start and maintain a successful business.

*Don't get obsessive about your competition.*

# SLOW DEATH BY EMAIL

There are two types of entrepreneurs: those who spend their days dealing with emails, and those who actually build great businesses. Rarely do the twain meet. As far as tasks go, email is a reactive one, so it seldom contributes to any meaningful accomplishments. You're not creating, you're *responding*. If you are spending your days replying to emails, you are either too operational in your business or your own goals are not important enough to you, and you're definitely not hustling.

Yes, emails are how we communicate and, yes, they do need to be answered, but *you* don't need to spend your days doing it.

So, what are you going to do about it? Firstly, delegate your emails to someone else who can handle most of them for you, and for the rest dedicate a certain time in the day for dealing with emails, preferably in the late afternoon when you no longer have to be razor sharp.

Secondly, turn off any email apps on your phone and disable any notifications. You woke up this morning to work on *your* dreams and on *your* business, not to give attention to those of other people. Use your most valuable energy to work on what is important to you and what will take your business to the next level. Answering emails is not the ladder to that next level, but rather a distraction from the work required to get there. (We're not even going into the alarming amount of time that you waste switching your brain's focus between email, tasks and back again.)

In the early days it was OK to respond when you were able to; people didn't think of email as an instant messaging application. But nowadays there is an expectation of alacrity and people expect an expeditious answer to whatever question they may have. But the interesting thing is this: they only expect it if you allow them to. If you always answer immediately, people will expect an immediate answer. If you don't, people are actually OK with it and the expectation is realigned.

Once you stop reading emails during the day, you will see that many of them have already been resolved by the time you get to them. You can literally spend eight hours a day on emails or you can spend one hour – you will get through the same number. The difference is the *results*.

Email: Stop doing it.

---

> *You can't afford to spend all your time answering emails.*

---

# RULE
## 26　STOP THE DIY

Emails aren't the only thing entrepreneurs have a hard time letting go of ... So many of us want to try to do everything ourselves. It's the greatest downfall in a lot of businesses today. It's only when your business stops growing and is no longer viable that you find yourself asking why you never sourced the necessary expertise to make things work earlier on.

Marketing, sales, product development, accounting and many more facets of a business become the responsibility of a new entrepreneur when starting out. But when we move to the next level, we're still trying to do it all. Why? To save on costs? Because nobody can do *anything* as well as you can? Let me remind you that your job is to *grow* the business, which you simply cannot do if you're still trying to *be* the business. So, are you going to continue to try to do everything yourself, or do you employ someone, or outsource the work to a business that can manage it for you?

As a start, these three tasks are the most easily outsourced:

- *Marketing*: Gone are the days of traditional marketing; everything is now digital. Google, Facebook and Instagram are among the best marketing programmes to utilise to get your product out there. Can you do it yourself? Yes, of course, but the right agency will do it *better*. You know your product best, but they definitely know how best to market it.

- *Legal*: When it comes to legal fees, businesses are often penny wise and pound foolish, resorting to downloading standardised templates from the Internet and retrofitting them to meet imminent business needs – essentially half-assing really important pieces of work. This can cost the business dearly in the long run when you get taken to task over faulty contracts, bad HR policies or illegal practices. Find an affordable expert or firm that can help you with the legal work and will be able to defend you in court if things go south, as well as advise you on the best ways to avoid ending up there in the first place.

- *Accounting*: You can outsource this task to experts who can advise you on how best to run your business, how to save on taxes and, most importantly, keep you on the right side of the law. Monthly accounting service packages are generally cheaper than employing your own internal accountant and come with a lot more expertise.

As entrepreneurs, we need to focus our time on where the money is and get the right experts to support us with other tasks. No man is an island.

---

*Focus your time on where the money is and get the right experts to support you.*

---

# RULE
## 27

# WELCOME THE AGE OF DIGITAL AUTOMATION

Ten years ago companies had to pay thousands to get desktop software and expensive servers to run their software. They had to employ developers to develop custom applications for unique tasks, all of which was impossible for the small business owner. But it's 2020 and the small business owner is in a totally different position now.

For a couple of hundred dollars a month, the SME can now have the best cloud based software to automate most of the tasks in the business, freeing up human capital to focus on human work and giving customers a better experience.

If you are an entrepreneur and you are not using great software at the moment, I hope this rule will make you reconsider it. It's faster, it's friendlier and it's far more efficient.

Here are a few applications that are changing the world for small businesses:

- *Xero*: Accounting software that can automate accounting tasks. It can send quotes and invoices to customers, follow up automatically on outstanding invoices, submit expense claims online and reconcile bank transactions automatically with live bank feeds.

- *Zoho*: There are a range of products from CRM to Support Desk applications that can make interactions easier. It can also custom-make applications through simple drag and drop options.

- *WooCommerce*: If you want to live online, this software can get an online shop running for you in less than an hour. Sell online, let customers place orders online and manage stock online.

- *Zapier*: This could win a prize for the best software ever created. It is a web automation app that allows you to automate parts of your business or personal life. It connects different applications and acts as a blueprint for a task you want to perform repeatedly.

These are just some of the many thousands of apps available for the small business. Whatever business you are in, and regardless of the problems you face, you will find software that can solve many of them for you. You just need to have an open mindset for change and the results will be magical.

---

*Free up human capital to do human work.*

---

# RULE
## 28 HOW TO BE LAZY

We all know the guy who is at the gym all the time. The one who checks in every single day and spends many, many hours there. And yet he is completely out of shape. He walks on a treadmill at a slow pace while scrolling Instagram. He talks to everyone. He always brags about his health but his physical state does nothing to back that up. He achieves nothing. Compare him with the guy who checks in for an hour, five days a week, but gives his everything. He is in shape, healthy and fit.

The time spent doing something is not directly proportional to the success you achieve from it. It's not 'how much time', but rather what you have *done* with that time.

Many entrepreneurs are in the same boat. They work crazy long hours yet they achieve very little. They spend their time on tasks that will take their business nowhere. Not only is this unproductive, but it is also demotivating.

Then there's the *amount* of time you spend on tasks, regardless of importance. Parkinson's Law postulates that 'work expands to fill the time available for its completion'. In real terms, this means that many people spend days on tasks that should only take a few minutes to complete because they've allowed for it, which is a waste of chronic proportions.

The sad part of it is that most of these entrepreneurs know that what they're doing may create the impression of hustle, but it isn't providing the lift they need, yet they'll keep doing it anyway. They know that being operational won't do anything for their business. They know that checking email all day won't move them forward. They know this, but it feels comfortable and the challenging tasks, the ones that will actually move the needle, are 'unknown' or 'uncomfortable'. Much like exercising.

How do you change this? You step back from your business before the day starts and you list the things that you need to do that will *actually* move the needle. Things that only *you* can do. Then you decide how long each should take to complete. Lastly, you stick to both criteria as if they were law. You don't do anything BUT this, and the value of the work should be measured in terms of results, not sweat. Hard work is useless when it is spent doing the wrong things.

Working smart is the only option for great entrepreneurs. The rest are doomed to the same fate as Sisyphus and his boulder.

---

*Hard work is useless when it is spent doing the wrong things.*

---

# RULE
## 29 YOU GET WHO YOU PAY FOR

Now that you have your big-boy pants on, it's time to look at those you surround yourself with. When you listen to entrepreneurs talk about their biggest mistakes, more than half the time they will say that they should have hired better people earlier on. Many simply don't know how to do it.

When you start out, you are the smartest person in your world and you can do everything yourself. You soon run out of time and you employ juniors (cheap labour), thinking you can train them – and you might be able to, but it will take a lot of your time and patience. You may get it right, or you will just give up and continue to do everything yourself. Either way it's a lot of input for rather meagre output.

Or you look at hiring smart people, but the salary expectations terrify you and you quickly back down. Some of them are asking for more than *you* earn. That will never happen.

But when you give this a go, you soon realise that it is these people who actually make your business grow exponentially. They are even better than you are. Yes, you pay them a lot but they are making you double, even triple, the money. Richard Branson is famous for realising this and using it to create many successful businesses.

The third option is cloning, and we're still a few years off from that. Even if we weren't, I wouldn't recommend it. People are more than just a way to do stuff you can't do any more, they bring interesting thinking and fresh ideas.

The best will even challenge your decisions, usually to the betterment of the overall business. In fact, I'd go as far as to say that the best thing about other people is that they're *not you*. Steve Jobs said, 'We hire smart people so they can tell *us* what to do.'

And it gets better. When you hire smart people, they will train your other staff as well as attract even *better* people. To grow a great business, you need to hire the best. They will come at a price but it is a price that is totally worth it.

You will realise that there are many people who are as smart as you are and when you have them on your team, you will have double the time, your profits will soar and you will have the money to pay even better employees. Don't skimp on it.

---

*To grow a great business, you need to hire the best.*

---

# RULE
## 30 TIME FOR AN OFFICE

The garage days are over; get yourself an office. This may be controversial and there's a lot of debate around it, especially as businesses are starting to move away from office spaces towards a 'work from anywhere' setup, but it made a big difference in most of the businesses I have worked with.

As a young entrepreneur, you need your team to be doing the heavy lifting for you. You can amplify this effect if you work together, and if they are in the same physical space it just makes everything so much easier. You can create a culture, you can get things done more quickly. Many entrepreneurs will testify how huge the growth in their business was when they moved to offices after trying it out in a virtual world.

Once you have nailed the business and your systems, you can allocate certain tasks to be done remotely and employees can work off site. You can have systems in place to monitor them and can use tools to ensure proper collaboration. But never forget that good stuff happens when people come together.

Obviously, there are exceptions to the rule. In certain industries, it will make sense to work remotely. If you can't hire good staff in your location, you might look to employing someone working overseas. For certain tasks, you may be able to get a better deal from outside employees. Those are the exceptions; in most cases, having your team close to you will ensure more rapid growth.

Many entrepreneurs have a hybrid approach. They hire an office once a week to get the team together to talk about what they are busy with, to plan for the week ahead, and to report back on the previous week's work. This allows the opportunity for the team to work together and resolve any issues that need to be attended to physically.

See what works for you – virtual, physical, or a bit of both.

---

*Good stuff happens when people come together.*

---

## RULE 31

# THE RIGHT FINANCING AT THE RIGHT TIME

Most aspiring entrepreneurs say that they don't have the capital they need to start their businesses, and blossoming businesses face the same challenge. No capital = no growth. While I honestly believe that there is every reason to avoid getting a loan, there are times when it's the only reasonable solution. But, even then, you have *options*.

An entrepreneur's first point of reference when looking for capital is the traditional banks. But let's be frank, banks don't readily give money to small businesses and, when they do, it's only when the business or the business owners can provide enough security. They *claim* to support small businesses and spend millions on marketing this, but they keep entrepreneurs on a line, constantly asking for more information, only to reject the application in the end. Very few banks will look at an entrepreneur's vision and plan as sufficient collateral.

But there are other options and, globally, more and more financial institutions are offering alternative financing products for businesses. The two most common ways to get finance include:

- *Purchase Order Finance*: When you are doing business with large companies, there are institutions that will advance you money upon receipt of orders from your customers.

These institutions know the orders are in good standing and they carry the risk of lending you the money to execute the order. Usually, financing is advanced upon the placement of the order and repayment is due when the client pays you. This is called financing against orders.

- *Invoice Financing*: You may also consider financing against invoices which works in a similar way to the above. Invoices to clients are often only paid after 30 days, if not longer. There are institutions that offer financing options to take over these invoices (or debtors) from you and pay you instantly. They charge a small percentage of the invoice amount but allow your business to operate and remove the burden and effort of collecting payments from customers.

If you own a good business, there's no reason why you shouldn't get financing. Perhaps traditional banks are to be avoided, but with other options out there, who needs 'em?

---

*Traditional banks are not your only source of capital.*

---

# RULE
## 32

# PUT ON A PAIR OF CUSTOMER-SIZED SHOES

We often become so immersed in our own product or service that we no longer consider that what *we* find special is not the same thing our customers are buying. We don't think like our customers. Or we forget how to. We see things simply as a supplier and can't understand why we don't find customers more easily, or why customers are unhappy with what we offer.

To turn this around, simply put yourself in your customers' shoes. You should do this not only when you sell to them, but also when you service them after a sale.

Customers may not know or understand technical terms that are applicable only to your industry, so don't focus on these things when you sell to them – they don't care how many subverted iconoprest flagilaters went into your solution. Customers often just want a basic problem solved, and they don't care how you do it. If, for example, you are a printing company providing printing services to small businesses, don't go to market declaring what amazing printers and inks you use, or how often you service your machines. Your customers aren't interested in that. They want great-looking printing as cheaply as possible accompanied by great service. Technical specifications are their last concern. When you talk to them, consider what *they* think is important – their buying motives – and build from there.

The same applies to operations. In the example on the previous page, the small business may need flyers printed for their upcoming conference at the weekend. They are under pressure and you, as a supplier, need to understand this and accommodate them as much as possible. Try to see how you can help them rather than bitching about 'company procedures'. Put yourself in your customers' shoes (all the time). How would you have felt if you were treated indifferently?

An important factor to consider is that things are changing. Something that worked or was relevant two years ago, might no longer be relevant. You need to evolve with your customer over time, as their expectations do. This will be even more important as millennials are rising and starting more and more businesses, and they think completely differently from people just a few years older than them.

Someone who grew up with a smartphone and tablet, who orders a pizza online and grabs a taxi on an app, won't be happy with your four-page application form that needs to be filled in and posted back before an account can be opened. They will find suppliers who are capable of supporting them in the way they want to do business.

Don't be arrogant. Address the problems of the people who pay you – your customers. If you don't, your competitors will.

---

*If you can't think like your customer, your competitors will.*

---

# RULE
## 33

# MAKE MARKETING MATTER

Marketing is so important that I'm sure if anyone else wrote a business book like this, they would include 30 rules on marketing alone. But I've never seen myself as a marketer because it's not something I understand intimately. I'm definitely able to do sales and close deals. I understand numbers and I can drive a strategy. *Those* are my strengths. I've always outsourced marketing to people who know what they're doing far better than I ever will.

That said, while you're still growing you may not have the budget for a proper marketing strategy, or the execution thereof. If this is you, you should look at digital marketing. I've created many businesses purely from online marketing. Your audiences and clients are most likely (read that as *definitely*) on Google and social media, and there are so many tools out there that can play the role of expert until you can afford a human one. As you build a brand, you want to be seen on magazine covers and TV, but this is just your ego talking. As a small business you should really only be interested in finding clients and closing deals. There is no better place to achieve this than on the Internet.

There is a *chance* that someone might browse through a magazine to pass the time, your advert *might* catch their attention and you *may* get a sale – but the hit rate is very low. Compare this to a user actively searching for your service or product on Google, and finding what they're looking for. Of course the chance of your making a sale will be more online advertising – if your digital presence is up to scratch. So where do you think is the best place to spend your marketing budget?

Most businesses today agree. The majority of their leads are being generated online so they're cutting their traditional media budgets. Marketers might disagree with me, but I can't see how these old legacy platforms are even going to be relevant in ten years' time if they don't change drastically. They are not as good and are more expensive – they can't survive. If you can afford it, I'd suggest finding a solid digital marketing agency to add the expertise and insights you need – the return will be well worth it.

As a small business looking for clients, don't even look at anything if you don't have a proper digital strategy in place.

---

*Don't even look at anything if you don't have a proper digital strategy in place.*

---

# DISTRACTION TO FOCUS

## BY ERIK KRUGER

*Erik started as a stranger, but he has subsequently become a very solid friend, and an exceptional entrepreneur. I helped him create his first blog, which ignited his addiction to all things online. Erik has written across various media on productivity, time-management, leadership, and better decision-making and, in the process, amassed a following of more than 80,000 people. Through his online platform, BetterMan, he works to help people make themselves unstoppable!*

The start of my entrepreneurial journey can be summarised in one word: *distraction*.

I realised soon after graduating as a physiotherapist that I did not actually want to be one. Instead, I wanted to build a successful online business. At the time I did not grasp the hard work and perseverance that would be needed to build a functioning business – never mind a wildly successful one!

So I tried to launch several businesses at the same time. In just a few years I had registered over forty domain names. Each time I registered a new one I thought to myself 'This will be the one!', but it never was. It became such a pattern that whenever I sat down for coffee with Marnus he always asked me, 'Which new domain have you registered today?' It was a joke at the time, but it was also a symptom of my inability to stick to one idea. Distraction was the name of the game; I could not stay focused long enough to allow my projects to gain traction.

In 2014 I decided to focus all my energy on one project alone. This felt unnatural, but it worked. I finally managed to gain traction, and build something that people wanted. It taught me a few rather important lessons:

1. *Focus*. Spend 100 per cent of your effort on launching one business. Diversify later.

2. *Be patient*. It's the last thing any entrepreneur wants to hear. But it's true. Do not become seduced by the perceived overnight success of others. They have all put in the hours. Guaranteed.

3. *Become skilled*. The years leading up to BetterMan were my formative years. They gave me the opportunity and time to teach myself how to do branding and marketing. This enabled me to become proficient at certain technical skills, such as designing and working with WordPress. They were all skills which came in handy when I finally launched BetterMan.

Entrepreneurs are always looking for the silver bullet – the short cut between starting up and success. It doesn't exist.

All that exists is *accretion* – the slow and steady accumulation of skills, experience and knowledge. This pattern can be seen when you dissect the lives of the greats. Over time this slow accumulation gains momentum and makes you unstoppable.

# THE RIGHT STEP AT THE RIGHT TIME

## Part 3: Scaling up. And up. And up

Creating scale in a business – allowing it to grow almost exponentially – is always one of the greatest challenges medium-sized businesses face. What you've got *works*, but it's not as easy as copy/pasting it elsewhere. If you truly want to grow in size and reach, you have to flip some things on their heads.

# RULE
## 35
# BIG ISN'T ALWAYS BETTER

This may be a strange notion with which to start this section, but it's something you need to hear.

You've heard people talk about being a 'big fish in a small pond', but few talk about how to move into a bigger pond so that you can grow. At this stage, doing more of the same will not get you more. The progression stops being linear, and something's gotta give. This is probably the most difficult place for a small business owner to be.

You've built your business on people, you've done most of the tasks yourself but you are restricted by time. You can't get to everything and things are falling through the cracks. You hire more people but they are (let's be frank) useless and can't do the job as well as you. The wheels start coming off ...

Small business owners in this space try hard to overcome the problem by throwing money and resources at the issues, which very seldom works. Profit decreases because of additional expenses, customers are not getting the service they used to and they depart. The business owner is in a dilemma: either I close the business or I scale down to a smaller business, one where I have fewer staff and fewer customers but I make more money, one where I manage everything myself and know that I will do a good job.

Sometimes the best thing to do is to make peace with the fact that you are never going to have a huge business, but at least it will be a manageable one. And that's OK! This suits some people better – folks who are more concerned with happiness than profits. The team is closer, and they tend to be more fun (to run).

The downside is that the business can never scale and will always depend on the owner to run things. Not a great business to sell one day, but a great business from which to earn a living and one with fewer immediate problems.

It is a path many choose and it is better than going under. But there is an alternative: building a business on systems (and not people) – see the next rule.

---

*It's OK if you'd rather stay small, manageable and hands on.*

---

# RULE
## 36 SCALING THROUGH SYSTEMS

'Behind every powerful man is a woman telling him what to do', but behind every big business is a system of systems that control the business. If you really want the business to climb to the next level, you are going to have to add systems, processes and procedures to manage what you will no longer be able to.

A different approach is needed – one where you document everything that needs to be done and how it needs to be done. You automate as far as possible and then you hire people to operate within the system. They should be able to take the operations manual and become experts.

The great businesses that are able to serve many customers and scale up from the intermediate level to the next did not get there by depending solely on people, but rather on systems operated by efficient people.

McDonald's is probably the best known example in the world of systems-based scaling. They managed to scale a restaurant making burgers to an empire serving millions of burgers a day because they did not depend on a great chef deciding each day how the burger should taste and how much salt should be used. They didn't leave service decisions up to servers, like other smaller restaurants do. 'Take these systems and execute them – no room for error.' Theirs is a great documented system, tried and tested, telling franchise owners and employees exactly what they should do and how they should do it. The recipe is a proven success and the moment anyone executes it exactly they, too, become successful.

Finding which systems to automate can be tricky because there are so many options for a medium-sized business. My advice would be to take a long hard look at what your business actually does – what your purpose is – and use that as a guide. Certain parts of your business don't need 'the human touch', so putting systems in place will make the entire business more efficient (like customer acquisition), while other parts are core to what you do differently, so flexibility may need to be retained for them to be most effective.

If you can reduce the load to 10 per cent of your business, by making them run at maximum efficiency, what could that do to your profits? If you can put a system in place that allows that part of your business to do the same thing, only faster, how much more can you squeeze from it? Don't sneeze at the power of cumulative accretion.

Small business owners don't want to think like this. They don't want to spend time stepping back and putting systems in place to make things easier. After all, it wasn't systems that got them where they are; instead they just keep charging forward until they burn out or decide to scale down.

If you want to play with the big boys, you have to adjust to a new set of rules.

---

*Great businesses scale up through systems operated by efficient people.*

---

# RULE 37

## ECONOMISING OR EXPANDING?

Earlier we spoke about 'not getting ahead of your success'. This rule changes significantly when you're trying to grow bigger than your boots. One of the biggest mindsets small business owners need to acquire is one of balance – the balance between not wasting money or spending unnecessarily and realising that *without* spending money they can't grow a bigger business.

Entrepreneurs don't want to hire more expensive staff, but do not realise that the expensive staff will allow their businesses to do bigger and better things. They don't want to spend money on marketing, but without spreading the word they are not going to grow their sales. They don't want to invest in software to solve problems, but don't realise that the problems are costing them more than the software.

Most small businesses are fighting for survival and owners are cutting costs wherever they can. They are hesitant to incur further costs and this is often the reason why a business stagnates. There is the (understandable) fear of risk: more marketing will bring in more sales, but there is an element of risk: what if it doesn't? What if the more expensive employee does not perform? What if the software doesn't work?

The approach needs to change: owners need to weigh up costs versus opportunity and make calculated decisions regarding the validity of those costs. But the reality is, and always will be, that you need to spend money to make money.

There are ways to minimise the spending as well as the risks. You could go for a smaller marketing campaign to test it before 'shooting the lights out'. You could hire a consultant on a part-time basis rather than as a full-time employee. Get software vendors to provide demos and guarantees before shelling out for the annual subscription.

There are other ways around the problem too, but the business owner will still need to make a shift in mindset: to grow a bigger business, I need to be willing to spend money. And when that mindset is shifted: how can I reduce my risks so that I do not waste money?

It's a balancing act, but one you need to come to grips with if you want to get where you need to be.

---

*Owners need to weigh up costs versus opportunity.*

---

# RULE
## 38

# KNOW WHEN TO FINANCE

Entrepreneurs are often faced with the question of whether or not they should go into debt in order to grow their businesses. There are times when it's simply impossible to use what you have to create the scale you need, and financing becomes the best option. But taking a loan is always a risky action, and it needs to be evaluated properly.

There are two specific times when existing businesses might need to look at taking a loan.

The first is when you're closing gaps. This is when you are running out of cash and you need to fund the company's overheads to keep going. This is a super risky exercise because, if you are not making enough money right now to fund overheads, how will you make enough money to fund them in the future, as well as repay the loan (with interest)? Or you may be in a position where you are busy with something big in the short term which will generate more sales in the future and a loan is needed to bridge this gap. Either way, cutting costs is a smarter call because it's less dangerous but, if you truly believe that something great is on the horizon, then a loan might be a viable option. Just make sure you have planned properly for this and that you have reduced your risks to the lowest possible level.

The second time a loan could work out favourably is when you need it to enable you to execute a big deal. This might come in the form of a big project that needs to be completed, or an import company might need cash to bring in a big shipment. This loan won't be to keep the business running, as in the previous example, but specifically to fund a particular project. Here you really need to understand the numbers; if you can calculate that the profit on this project will be more than the interest on the loan, then it will be worth it for you and there is no reason not to gear such growth.

In short, if the loan will enable you to create a substantial return, and the likelihood of that return actually happening is high, it is common sense to proceed. The important thing here is to have a plan, to understand the numbers and then make sure that you execute the plan.

---

*Taking a loan is always a risky action, and it needs to be evaluated properly.*

---

# THE THREE PILLARS THAT SHAPED OUR SUCCESS

## BY MARK FORRESTER

*You may not know Mark, who is possibly one of the biggest success stories in South Africa, but you'll definitely be aware of the things he's created. A few years ago he turned from web-designer to web-entrepreneur when he founded WooThemes, a business that creates WordPress themes for people all over the world, and then WooCommerce, the most customisable ecommerce platform, which now powers almost 40 per cent of all online stores. Every time we hook up over a coffee I'm reminded of how humble Mark is, and how much insight he has into the entrepreneurial landscape.*

In 2007 I rather serendipitously connected with two strangers, both living in other countries, who shared a similar passion to me. We founded a company together called WooThemes. Eight years later we sold our company to WordPress, a billion dollar tech enterprise that is responsible for powering over 25 per cent of the Internet.

When I think back over our whirlwind journey I can identify three pillars that shaped our success.

1. *We found a niche within a niche*

   WooThemes built off-the-shelf website templates for a platform called WordPress. Back then, WordPress was a simple blogging platform that predated Twitter. It was a time when people shared thoughts and moments, unconstrained by a character count, in journal format on personal websites that they owned. Today, WordPress has evolved into a fully fledged content management system and powers tens of millions of websites. It has a very active and enthusiastic community of users and builders.

   We were fortunate to discover a need within this large existing user base, and there was no reason to reinvent the wheel.

   WordPress was our niche, and we were going to help make it more beautiful via off-the-shelf templates. We were calculated in our approach in what to build and how to target customers.

2. *We grew our personal brands and leveraged others*

   Our go-to market strategy was simple: build as many templates, for as many niche usages of WordPress as possible. From personal blogs to news publications and from photography sites to real estate listings.

   All three of us had existing audiences following our personal blogs, and we'd built up our reputations as go-to designers for WordPress custom design and development work. This was a good launch pad for our offering. We also harnessed the reputations and influence of other movers and shakers within the web design world and got them also to design templates for us. We paid these designers once-off contract fees and took care of all the development ourselves. These designers proudly showcased their work to their blog audiences and our net was cast even wider.

Within a few weeks of these templates launching, sales grew and the products became profitable. WordPress folk were happy because they could now gain access to web design resources previously restricted to those with deep pockets.

3. *We embraced open-source*

WordPress is open-source, meaning anyone can view and modify the code behind the platform.

This is somewhat anti-establishment when you think of the walled gardens that the rest of the Internet exists within today. Open-source is, however, more than a code licence. It's a hugely powerful, knowledge-sharing philosophy that is bigger than the Internet itself.

By 2012, our WooThemes offering grew from off-the-shelf templates into providing an ecommerce solution for WordPress. Our customers were asking for templates with shopping cart features. Shop functionality for WordPress was very limited and complex, so we set out on a quest to build the functionality ourselves. We called this new offering WooCommerce.

Over the years we'd grown to support a large community of developers and designers, using our products as their building blocks for client work. We provided entrepreneurial opportunity. These community members were very keen to help us build, grow and market WooCommerce. WooCommerce succeeding meant that their tool kit grew bigger.

WooCommerce has grown into an ecommerce platform that is used by nearly two million websites – over 40 per cent of all online shops.

When you can help support success for others, your success is imminent.

# THE RIGHT STEP AT THE RIGHT TIME

## Part 4: Getting ready to sell

Not everyone *wants* to sell their business. For most, there are years of so much blood, sweat and tears that offloading it is tantamount to killing a part of oneself. But there are others who built their businesses specifically for this purpose, and others still who have hit a juncture in their lives where it's time to do 'something else'. This short section will hopefully provide a little insight for those who see their future elsewhere.

# RULE
## 40

# KNOW WHAT YOU'RE GETTING INTO

Some entrepreneurs are 'starters', they like to start a business, get it off the ground and then flog it. Others are 'growers', they look for existing businesses and have the ability to grow them beyond their original value. Both will probably get to the same end point: selling the business.

But entrepreneurs are often misled when it comes to the sale. They have put everything into the business and it is worth a huge amount to them because of it. But buyers are seldom willing to match the price, *because what is being sold, and what is being bought, are not the same thing.* Sellers see the emotional and financial investments they've put in; the buyer mostly looks at one thing: profit. Effort does not equal profit. The balance is out.

How do you get your business to market? The owner of a small business can advertise the business for sale, make contact with other businesses to find out if they might be interested in a takeover, or even appoint a business broker to act as an agent and sell the business on your behalf (they will manage the entire process and take a commission, usually 10-15 per cent). All of the above have associated pros and cons and *all* of them will have their own best interests at heart, not yours. Remember that.

Once you get to market you will also realise that there are, unfortunately, fewer buyers than you'd like ... Unlike listed companies, you can't sell shares easily and quickly on a public platform. Instead, you need to find an interested individual or business, many of whom just aren't buyin' what you're sellin'.

Some of them are, but that doesn't guarantee a sale. Most small businesses must put their faith in a cash deal, since banks will never finance anyone wanting to buy them. In reality, this means that you may have a genuinely interested buyer for your business, who won't be able to get finance for it from the bank (who are great at making promises they know they won't deliver on). So, after a few months, you're back to square one. After a few rounds of this cycle many entrepreneurs will just sell out of desperation, forgetting what the business could actually be worth.

Selling a business can be very emotionally draining and this will be compounded by many people who will waste your time and mess you around. You spent a large portion of your life building this, but others will not see it the same way you do. Ensure that you prepare and mitigate against all of those issues, and have the stomach for the fight.

If you are considering selling your business, ensure that you do your homework. Get your business into a good state for a sale and be realistic in terms of the price you can expect. See the next two rules for more about these.

*Entrepreneurs are often misled when it comes to the sale.*

# RULE
## 41 BEING PREPARED TO SELL

If you are looking at exiting your business, it is crucial to allow enough time to prepare yourself for it. Maybe you're simply tired of your business and you just want to get out but, because the business is not in a great state at the moment, you're too fed up to care, and you simply don't have the energy to fix the issues. You're at risk of letting your business go for next to nothing. All the hard work for hardly any reward ...

If you have the end in mind, and *prepare* for it, it can be a very different, more lucrative story.

A successful transaction will mostly boil down to having a solid business with great systems in place that is making decent money and the starting point for these transactions will be financial information. You need to have proper financial records for your business and you need to be able to show the potential buyer how much the business is making and how it is making it. It sounds so elementary yet most entrepreneurs don't have financial information when they want to sell their businesses. If you think you may want to sell in the future, make sure you're keeping solid records *now*.

If your business's financials are messy, start cleaning them up at least twelve months before trying to sell your business. Remove all your personal expenses from the business and ensure that all transactions are properly recorded, and that your taxes are up to date and accurate. Work with your accountant to prepare a sales pack with all your financial information, including details of your clients, employees, suppliers, what your strong and weak points are and how the business could grow in the future. It's at this stage that you can pick up on issues and resolve them before taking your business to the market, making it a much more attractive product.

With some (more) hard work, you will be in a great position to sell your business, you will have serious buyers and the valuation that you deserve for all your hard work. If you don't, why bother?

---

*A successful transaction will mostly boil down to having a solid business with great systems in place.*

---

# RULE
## 42 UNDERSTANDING THE 'VALUATION' IDIOM

There is so much BS going around when it comes to business valuations and what entrepreneurs can expect when selling their businesses, and one half of it contradicts the other half. The tech industry created a perception that if you have an idea half executed, you can sell it for billions but, in anything other than extreme cases, this is about as far from reality as you can get without going over the edge of the world ...

Although there are many factors to be considered when putting a valuation on a business, it will mostly be determined by your *profit*. There are exceptions, again especially in the tech industry, where intellectual property (IP) and number of customers are more important, but only because the IP and customers will contribute substantially to that profit in the future. Numbers are everything.

Like anything economic, the actual sale of a business depends on two parties: a willing buyer and a willing seller. These two parties need to meet halfway and both need to be happy with a valuation. Sometimes sellers are lucky, they get the right buyer willing to pay a premium price; most times they are not lucky. In fact, more often than not it's only the buyer who walks away whistling.

When trying to sell a business in its startup phase, before it has made any profit, it is almost impossible to have a template for a valuation. The seller needs to work on assumptions and sketch a picture of how the business will look when it is successful, and the buyer needs to buy into this plan. There is really no formula; it is completely subjective.

When it comes to more established businesses, it is much easier to calculate a valuation. For this, many entrepreneurs often go to accountants who will apply some proprietary algorithm and come back with a ridiculously unrealistic amount. They completely ignore what price the market is willing to pay for said business.

Let me drop some simple knowledge: the average small business in the UK can expect to get a valuation of around three times their annual profit (also referred to as a PE of 3). So, if the business is making £1 million per year, the average valuation will be around £3 million. There are exceptions, but this would be the average in most industries.

As businesses get bigger, this number will increase – the average PE of FTSE-listed companies in the UK is currently sitting on 17.

As a seller, your expectations should be grounded in reality – value, as well as market sentiment. But remember what it is you're getting rid of, and make sure it's worth it, regardless of what your accountant tells you.

---

*Make sure your business is worth its value, regardless of what your accountant tells you.*

---

# 3

# HUSTLE. HUSTLE. HUSTLE. HUSTLE. THEN KEEP HUSTLING

It's my mantra for life – hustle. Hustle is about making things happen, not accepting the status quo, and pushing harder every day. Easier said than done, right? These are some of the ways I think you can bake a little hustle into your entrepreneurial life.

# RULE
## 43

# SIZE THE PRIZE

Michael Mendelowitz is one of the founders of Transaction Capital (a JSE-listed company worth millions) who bought a stake in The Beancounter in 2016. He is another example of an 'under-the-radar' superstar entrepreneur, and he always preaches about one thing: size the prize. By putting in the same amount of energy, hours and money, one entrepreneur can build a million- or a billion-pound business – and it's not dependent on anything other than the opportunity. Some opportunities will keep you busier than the devil on judgement day but make you very little money, while others will make you more money than the Kardashians with the same or less effort.

Let's see how this works. Let's look at two construction companies – we'll call them Judgement Day Construction and Kim's Logistics. Kim's builds shopping centres and charges £10m per project, while Judgement Day helps with residential renovations for £20,000 per project. Which one is likely to create more financial success? Obviously, Judgement Day will need more clients, more employees, better systems, and more management to get even *close* to Kim's level – all of which equates to more time, money and energy. Which one would you rather be involved in? The one that demands piles of effort but returns divot-sized profits? Didn't think so.

Size the prize! The same entrepreneur who is great at selling to consumers will make much more money selling diamonds or high-value properties than selling pot plants.

Look at the opportunities presented, and evaluate them in terms of what you'll put in versus what you'll get out. More often than not, doing less of more is the smarter way to go.

---

*Doing less of more is the smarter way to go.*

---

# RULE
## 44     FIND YOUR BO

BO has nothing to do with the way you smell after a tennis match in November, but rather it's about your *Biggest Opportunity*. The proverb goes: *The man who chases two rabbits, catches neither*. And this applies in the business world. Entrepreneurs can easily become involved in too many different opportunities. Of course, as an entrepreneur that is part of your DNA: when you see a problem – and there are a *lot* of them – you want to solve it. The result is that you get involved in too many ventures at the same time.

The world has made us believe that 'serial entrepreneurs' are the ultimate success, but we assume that they ran their businesses in *parallel,* rather than sequentially. They don't. Most serial entrepreneurs start a business, focus on it exclusively, make a success of it and only then move on to the next big thing.

Parallel entrepreneurs are the ones juggling many businesses simultaneously. It might sound impressive when you hear about their ten businesses but they very seldom succeed in making any of them a huge success (never mind all of them). The reason more people don't juggle is because we don't like dropping things – more so where valuable businesses are concerned.

In business, focus is everything. You need to give all your attention and energy to one business, and its problems, at a time. Can you imagine how distracting it would be to simultaneously handle eight different businesses' different problems?

Think about what your **biggest opportunity** is – your BO –
and chase it relentlessly.

(As a side note, when you are in your existing business it
will always seem difficult and the next opportunity will
always seem easier – until you embark on it and then it,
too, will become challenging and you will again jump to the
next one.)

Don't make that mistake. Find your BO and pursue it from
morning to night.

---

*Find your* **biggest opportunity** *and*
*pursue it from morning to night.*

---

# RULE
## 45

# THE POWER OF 'NO!'

How often have you heard that you should say 'yes' to everything and then figure it out later? This is wrong – for many reasons. The greatest example in modern business is Steve Jobs. When he returned to Apple (the company he founded, and was fired from), it was struggling but Jobs turned it around by deciding to focus on just a few products and let go of all the rest. By way of explanation, he said, 'People think focus means saying yes to the thing you've got to focus on. But that's not what it means at all. It means saying no to the hundred other good ideas that there are. You have to pick carefully. I'm actually as proud of the things we haven't done as the things I have done. Innovation is saying no to 1,000 things.' And he was right.

To build a successful business, you need focus, which means saying no to many more things than you will say yes to.

There are many things to say NO to that would do us far more harm than good. Say NO to anything that won't contribute to what you want to achieve. Say NO to meetings that won't add value to your life or business. Say NO to jobs that aren't profitable because you should be finding ones that are. Say NO to the employee who always wants you to look at 'this one thing, really quickly' fifteen times a day. Say NO to friends who you don't really want to see. Say NO to that 'opportunity' that gives you a funny feeling. Say NO to cheap whisky!

And how do you say NO politely? You don't need to. You don't need to give a reason for not doing anything. You are an entrepreneur and you live life on your own terms. You are on a mission and you don't need to explain yourself.

The world is already full of YES-men. If you want to be a success, learn the power of NO, and how to say it *loudly*. Life's too short to do it any other way.

More on this in the next rule.

---

*Be as proud of the things you haven't done as the things you have done.*

---

# RULE
## 46

# KILL YOUR DARLINGS

The Pareto Principle (also known as the 80/20 rule, the law of the vital few, or the principle of factor sparsity) states that, for many events, roughly 80 per cent of the effects come from 20 per cent of the causes. It claims to be true for every aspect of life, and I don't think it is anywhere more true than in business.

It has become a common rule of thumb and every entrepreneur should know this and apply it wherever they can.

What does it mean in business?

- 80 per cent of your sales come from 20 per cent of your clients.
- 80 per cent of your problems come from 20 per cent of your clients.
- 20 per cent of your products contribute to 80 per cent of your sales/profit.

If this is true (and it is), how can you manipulate it to build a bigger and better business?

Determine which products or services generate the most income (the 20 per cent) and drop the rest (the 80 per cent) that provide only marginal benefits. *Just do it*. Be cold. Spend your time working on the parts of the business that you can improve significantly with your core skills and leave the tasks that are outside your best 20 per cent to other people. Work hardest on elements that work hardest for you. Reward the best employees well, fire the worst. Drop the bad, time-consuming, painful clients and focus on upselling and improving service to the best clients. After all, they're the ones who deserve your loyalty.

Imagine a business in which you spend 20 per cent of your time but get the same reward as if you spent all your time on it. Now, of course, as an entrepreneur, you aren't going to stop there. You will double the 20 per cent and thereby double your bottom-line.

It's so easy – but why is it so difficult to implement? Because, as humans, we tend to hang on to everything, especially things we worked hard at. Within that soon-to-be-discarded 80 per cent are many things that we love, and are proud of, as well as people we like. Stop looking at your business in terms of emotional attachments; see them rather as financial liabilities. *Which is what they are.* Be cold about it. Kill your darlings!

We think that the more we have, the wealthier we are. Scrap that. Much of what you have are anchors that are stopping you from building a great business.

---

*Focus on the parts of your business that deserve your loyalty.*

---

# RULE
## 47  5 MINUTES OR BUST

Whenever you don't feel like doing something, make an agreement with yourself that you will do it for just five minutes. Then hustle it for those measly 300 seconds. When the timer sounds and you don't feel like continuing, allow yourself to quit.

The rationale behind this is that starting is always the most difficult part of any task, but once you get past that initial intro you may find that the process is actually enjoyable and you are happy to continue. Human brains get so worked up about doing a simple thing that we will spend ten times more time thinking about doing it than actually just getting it done. This is something you would never have known if you didn't just get to it, which you wouldn't have done if you hadn't given yourself an 'out' to make sure you did!

The next time you don't want to go to the gym, agree on this rule. Get dressed, get into the car, check in and start to train. Five minutes later, you will most probably carry on. If not, pack up your stuff and leave.

Adopt the same approach in business. Start the proposal you've been deferring for months. If you don't want to carry on after five minutes, quit.

If it wasn't for this five-minute rule in my own life, you would not have been reading this book. It works. Wanting to write a book and actually *doing* it are completely different (as I found out). So, when I began, I did so by giving myself just 5 minutes of writing that I had to complete. And here we are, 46 rules later.

> *Often the hardest part of anything is the first 5 minutes.*

# RULE
## 48

# 10 MINI-RULES

## BY ROMEO KUMALO

*Before founding investment enterprise group Washirika Holdings, Romeo was the COO of Vodacom. He's a venture capitalist, has been involved with more boards than a surfing shop and was a Shark on Shark Tank South Africa, which was where we first met. He is honestly one of the nicest people in the world – ask anyone. But being nice doesn't make him any less worthy of respect in this space: these are his 10 mini-rules for entrepreneurs.*

1. *Don't take yourself too seriously*

   Life is already serious enough. It is imperative to have some fun along the way in order to lighten the journey towards success. If you believe in yourself, and your abilities, then success will follow, so there is no need to be serious all the time.

2. *Surround yourself with people who are better than you, people who are masters in their field*

   As an entrepreneur you don't have to know everything about all things. You will be more successful if you surround yourself with people who know everything that you don't know. Surround yourself with good people who can help you succeed and whose skills and way of doing business you admire.

3. *Live a life (and do business) of purpose and meaning*

   Live life according to your beliefs and values and do business that resonates with the same set of beliefs and values. Strive always to leave the world in a better condition than you found it. Always aim to give back to the community, invest in others, share your knowledge and help others grow.

4. *Do what you love and pursue your passion*

   If you are inspired from within, you will never run out of the energy to achieve your goals.

5. *There is no way to achieve success other than by working hard. You have to do the time*

   Don't try to cut corners. Short cuts won't help you on your path to success. Be prepared to put in the hours and make the necessary sacrifices to succeed.

6. *It is hard work but it is worth it*

   Achieving any success comes with hard work and perseverance. It won't be an easy ride but it will be well worth it when you achieve what you set out to do.

7. *Respect and gratitude*

   Be someone who is respectful of others. Show gratitude for all that was given to you along the journey towards success. Always remember those who made time for you, who helped you along the way. Say thank you and be respectful of the time that others have given to help you succeed.

8. *Reflect, re-evaluate, reassess*

   Regularly make time to reflect, re-evaluate and reassess where you are in your business, who you are as a person, who you do business with, what your success has been and what still needs to be done. Review your goals and your plans in order to stay relevant and successful.

9. *Educate yourself*

Always strive to know more. Educate yourself both formally and informally. Be an entrepreneur who is both book-smart and street-smart. If you know more, you can be more.

10. *Pass it forward*

Do unto others, as you would have liked to be done to you. If you can make someone else's path to success easier than yours was, do it. Return the favour of all that was invested in you to those who need it. Open doors for others and help them succeed.

# 4

# IT'S NOT JUST ABOUT YOU

I wish I could email those five words to every employer in the world, every day. If you want to create something amazing you need to realise that, at some stage, you'll need to bring others along with you. Those people will have your back and support you, and do the things you can't. But if you hire the wrong people to do the work, or treat the right people badly, there may not be much work left to do. It's not just about you.

# RULE
## 49 CULTURE ISN'T JUST FOR YOGHURT...

If you can get the best people on your team you will have a huge advantage over your competition. Skilled, motivated, awesome employees are the reasons you can do the big meetings and go for the big jobs. They are the reasons that you know you can cash the cheques that your mouth writes. Sometimes it's just enough that good people make all the hard work worth it. But getting those staff is about more than just a market-related salary – people seek a good environment to work in and one where they will be stimulated. One where they will be happy.

The great businesses of the future will not be the ones that pay the biggest salaries, but those that build the best cultures. Those businesses will attract the best talent. The best talent will attract the best clients. The best clients will give you the most money.

But what is culture and how do you build it? That's tricky, because most cultures developed, and were nurtured, they sure as heck weren't created. Culture is everything about the business and how the people in the business work together. It is the unspoken agreement on how clients are handled, or how people talk to each other. On what time it's acceptable to get to work, and when to leave. It's 'how we do stuff around here'. We all know those companies where employees are too afraid to talk, and companies where unethical events happen on a daily basis. We also know the companies where the staff work together, where they share ideas and problems, where they remember one another's birthdays. Both the positive and negative examples are all 'culture'.

Nowadays, people hire consultants to build cultures, to draft plans and to train employees. There is a simpler (and more honest) way, which is *by example*. It should happen organically, from the top down, be ingrained at every turn. Then you won't need textbooks, consultants or training sessions. Culture will happen automatically, and it will be real (really good, or really bad) and YOU will be responsible for it. People will take their lead from you, and replicate that.

If your door is always closed, you can't expect your senior staff to be helpful towards their juniors. If you think it is OK to forge a client's signature on a document, you can't be upset when fraud occurs in your business. It's all up to you.

My advice? Create the place you would want – no, *love* – to be employed in.

*Create a culture that you would want to be a part of.*

# RULE
## 50

# NO JOB DESCRIPTION GREY AREAS

One of the best ways to ensure calm and tranquillity at work, and to build a solid culture, is to make sure there's a shared understanding of expectations. If you are running a proper business, I would assume that you have proper agreements with all your staff (not only is it a basic requirement but it is also a law that you need to comply with) but, if you don't, download a template from a proper source or, even better, get a labour consultant to help you draft one. Right now.

In a basic agreement, you will include a job title and a job description, but these titles and descriptions are vague at best. Most tasks are assigned to employees verbally and it is expected that they will carry them out. Some will, but many won't, and this will mean huge frustration for the entrepreneur. It's not their fault you weren't explicit about what you wanted from them.

There is a basic solution. For every employee in your company (and yes, I said EVERYONE – from the cleaner to the CEO) draft another agreement, but this time make it an *operational* one. Create a one-pager with all the tasks they need to carry out (in detail), list everything you expect from them and get them to sign it. If they're not 100 per cent clear about everything, spend time explaining and discussing it. It need not be a formal agreement, but it has to happen. This is your 'shared understanding'.

Then when they don't do something, you can revisit the 'agreement' to see if the task was clearly outlined or if you maybe made an 'assumption'. Let it be a dynamic document and change it as required. You will soon find that many of your problems disappear.

Most employees want to do whatever is expected of them, but mostly they don't know what this is. A separate informal operational agreement listing their tasks and responsibilities will resolve the issue.

Try it, and you might just find out that people are not as stupid as you thought they were – the problem was actually the way you managed it.

*It's not your employees' fault if you're not clear about expectations.*

# RULE
## 51 LESSONS FROM AN OLYMPIAN

### BY RYK NEETHLING

*I first came into contact with South Africa's Olympic hero on a TV show we were both involved in. After destroying swimming records, he became a shareholder of, and the marketing director for, a luxury property developer in Franschhoek. His entrepreneurial spirit is what has allowed him to achieve so much: he will tell about how his life changed the day his team won gold in Athens, but how nobody considers 20 years of the hardest work imaginable that it took to get them there.*

These are the lessons I learned in my sporting career, that I still apply in my everyday life:

- Dream big and set clear goals often – DAILY!
- Don't be afraid of failure
- Be a champion on your worst day – CONSISTENCY!
- Be part of a team. Let me elaborate on this ...

It is quite interesting that I have such an affinity for teamwork considering swimming can sometimes be such a lonely, individual sport. The fact is that even in an individual sport it is impossible to get to the top without a strong team around you. Your coach, family and friends are all part of your team. I was fortunate to be part of two special teams in my career, one of them being the Olympic gold medal winning relay team in Athens in 2004, which changed my life forever. I am a big believer in surrounding yourself with positive, passionate experts in their field who provide the skills I don't have. You can't do everything. It takes some skill to assemble the right team and to get them to work towards a common goal but I can bear testimony to the results. It was in a team that I made my breakthrough as a swimmer, after which the individual honours followed. The same goes for business. The team in my world today consists of my partners, consultants, employees, mentors, family and friends. I could not do half as much without them.

# STATUS MEETINGS ARE CRUCIAL

A great routine to instil in your business is the habit of having 'status meetings' – a weekly meeting that takes place on the same day, at the same time. You can discuss whatever you want in this meeting and you can involve whoever you want. The idea is to have a dedicated time in the week with your team to get feedback from everyone, to align thoughts and to plan for the week ahead.

Such meetings bundle all the random day-to-day items of concern into one consolidated bundle, and will teach your employees to hold back on anything that isn't critical during the week and to deal with it when everyone is present. This will free you up to spend time on the important tasks instead of having to deal with small issues all the time, or having random meetings throughout the week. It also makes sure that you can see any issues in context, and see the links between them, which is difficult if they're all addressed ad hoc.

Status meetings are a great way to align everyone with what is happening in the business and what they need to be aware of, what keeps the team together and united around a singular purpose. It allows them to share problems and challenges, learn from one another, bond around the business.

These meetings keep employees accountable because they know they need to give feedback on the tasks they had during the week; nobody wants to be the only person who didn't deliver on their promises. For the same reason status meetings will keep you accountable to them, and to your business.

You could even lengthen this meeting to have standard recurring updates with other important people in your business: your accountant, suppliers or key customers.

The agenda will be different for every entrepreneur and every business, so you need to design a meeting around your business and your key performance indicators and then review them as you progress.

Status meetings are the best way to keep your business on track by keeping your people on track, but there's a small caveat: structure them before they happen, so there's an agenda which will stop them from going on for longer than they need to.

---

*A status meeting is a weekly meeting that takes place on the same day, at the same time.*

---

# RULE

## 53 YOUR PEOPLE MUST REPLACE YOU

One of the biggest mistakes we've all made is being too operational. We all know that entrepreneurs need to work more ON their businesses than IN their businesses, but I want to take it a step further: I think entrepreneurs should not work in their businesses at all. Start it, figure it out and understand it. Then document it, automate it and then *employ the right people to drive it for you*. These people, properly trained, will be your eyes, ears and hands working within the business while you're out expanding it.

This is another rule that most understand but don't follow. I know it's hard to let go, but it should only be so if you're worried about who's running the show. To avoid this, you need to empower your employees by giving them clear and detailed instructions and then let them get on with the work (status meetings are great for this). Don't micro-manage them but work continuously on the systems that will make their tasks easier. If you are continually interfering you will soon be left with employees who won't make decisions and won't take the initiative to start anything without you. The end goal is to create little clones of yourself who understand and believe in the business as much as you do. You want to create a system of like-minded people, supported by procedure, that will run by itself *as if you were in the same room*.

You need to replace yourself, and let employees deal with your business's day-to-day running. You can spend your time getting big deals, working on relationships with suppliers and clients, and working to improve the systems and processes. This way you will have a great business that is independent of you – that's a business that can scale and a business with real value when it comes to selling.

---

*It's hard to let go, but it should only be so if you're worried about who's running the show.*

---

# RULE
## 54 BE CAREFUL WITH YOUR NUMBERS GUY

Finding an accountant is usually the last thing on a new entrepreneur's list. And rightly so; there's a heck of a lot to do to create the numbers before you find someone to look after them. You need to start your business, get the paperwork done, find customers, prove your business model. But you'll get to a point where you're making enough money to be concerned about tax, Excel no longer works for invoicing, and the bank wants to see financials. An accountant is needed.

Be very careful. Not all accountants (and I speak as one of them) are created equal.

You may be expecting an individual (or company) who has the skills to justify their big (and often unexpected) bills and a partner who will help you grow your business. But most will just keep you compliant by swaddling you with red tape and delivering a reactive service, adding next to zero value. They force you to use old legacy systems and they make you stay with outdated processes. Their motivations are counter to your own.

The people you pay to help you grow can actually be the weeds that throttle you.

You need an accountant, but you need to find the right one. You need an accountant who will help set up a great system for you and work *with* you on this system (in real time), an accountant who will help you, be your trusted adviser and professional friend.

Once this is achieved, the magic happens: all your red tape is automatically taken care of and you can use the technology to grow your business and create an amazing experience for your customers, as well as having a professional who can guide you with numbers, business plans and the best tax advice.

Accountants can be an entrepreneur's best friend and trusted adviser but, more often than not they're little more than a grudge purchase. Find someone who really helps you, don't be shy about paying a slightly higher fee. Sit down for coffee or a beer before you draw up contracts. Tell them about your business and see what excites them. If you get this right they might just end up being the flywheel that spins your company's growth upwards.

---

*The people you pay to help you grow can actually be the weeds that throttle you.*

---

# RULE
## 55

# CELEBRATE THEIR SUCCESSES

We are so often preoccupied with chasing targets, leads and deadlines that we seldom stop to celebrate our achievements, or the achievements of those around us. We set great goals and expectations and we hustle hard to achieve them, and then we just move on as though nothing happened. We hardly acknowledge success as we start focusing on the next target.

This needs to change, not only for your own sanity but also to keep you and your team motivated. Your employees work hard – often harder than you realise – to achieve the target or goal that you set them. They are excited when they reach a milestone, but it is quickly downplayed by management focusing on the next thing. Their triumphs are forgotten, or treated as a basic part of their jobs. And, no, their salary is *not* reward enough. This attitude is demotivating and is one of the easiest ways to kill any remaining enthusiasm for your vision.

Make a point of celebrating all things – big and small. It's often the cheapest way to make better, happier, more motivated employees. It's like morale rocket fuel that will push your business ever onwards. Instil small things in your business culture to celebrate both individual and group success. Many sales teams keep a bell in their office and whenever they make a deal, the dealmaker rings the bell and the entire team celebrates. I knew another company that kept a book in which staff nominated their peers for doing something 'above and beyond', which was then rewarded and applauded by management once a week. It might seem a small thing but the effect on staff morale is massive.

Do the same in your personal life: work hard but reward yourself even harder. Set a tricky target and then take yourself to the Maldives when you reach it. You deserve every moment of it. We don't work this hard just to work even harder. We work hard to celebrate success. And the success is often less about the destination than it is about the journey.

*Celebrating is often the cheapest way to make better, happier, more motivated employees.*

# RULE

## 56 GIVE CREDIT WHERE IT'S DUE

This is an extension of the previous rule, but they're not quite the same. This one is about *ownership*.

I have seen far too many entrepreneurs who take the credit for the successes in their business as if they were the ones who were solely responsible for them. Just because your employees did it for you, and are employed by you, doesn't mean you get to pin it to your own jacket. Put your ego to one side and realise that, while you may have started the business, the reason it's still around is because of others. Your business is not all about you.

Everyone has a desire to be acknowledged and valued, and this goes beyond financial compensation. They want to be seen for what they are – contributors and collaborators.

One of the main reasons that employees resign is due to a lack of credit. When they feel that they are not being recognised for the work that they do, they become disheartened and they leave. There is nothing worse for a team than to realise that someone else is taking the credit for the hard work they have put in – don't be that guy.

Remember that, as an entrepreneur, you can't do it alone, and you are dependent on your team to make your vision succeed. Crediting your team as and when they perform is crucial in keeping them. This can be done in public or in private – but make sure you do it. It might not be a big deal for you, but it will mean the world to the people you do it for.

Also look at your managers and ensure that they are giving credit to the juniors under them. Recognition is infectious and contributes greatly to having a good company culture.

Make it a daily habit to compliment, thank and credit people around you. You will see how their faces light up and how much it means to them. You, in turn, will feel equally good and will soon have a highly motivated team willing to climb mountains for you.

---

*One of the main reasons that employees resign is due to a lack of credit.*

---

# RULE
## 57
# INCENTIVISE

Corporates are traditionally good at incentive drives. They implement programmes to push staff on performance or targets to be achieved by the company. This practice achieves two big objectives: employees know exactly what the target is, and they work harder and smarter to achieve it knowing that there's something in it for them.

Sales teams are used to this. The business's break-even figure is, well, *broken down*, and used to calculate how much each sales person needs to contribute to achieve it. Sales people are given targets and when they achieve them they will get a bonus commission. The big picture is filled in by smaller pieces, each of which has a carrot attached to it, increasing the likelihood of its coming to fruition.

Small businesses need to look at this more closely – not just for salespeople, but for everyone. Look at ways in which you can link your business's goals to small stop-gaps that employees can achieve, then find motivations for them to do so. See if you can get KPIs (key performance indicators) for every employee in your organisation that push them to grow themselves, and find out how you can incentivise them to perform better.

Don't have the mindset that incentivising staff will eat into your profits. Incentives work like an investment. As such, it's fairly easy to work out incentives for salespeople; if they bring in £10,000 of sales and you make 50 per cent profit on them, then it's logical to give them a 10 per cent commission.

Apply this to your operational team as well. What if they increased customer satisfaction so much that your customers are spending more money with you? Or they looked after your customers to such a degree that you don't lose any of them? Think about these issues and how you can reward your operational team.

We revolutionised the accounting industry by doing a couple of smart things and one of the smartest things was to reward our staff properly. We gave account managers commission on the clients they managed. If they got their systems working efficiently, they could take on more clients and earn more commission. If they serviced their clients well, they wouldn't lose them – more money for them.

There is something very special about running a business where everyone feels it in their pockets if a client decides to leave or someone doesn't pay their bill. Suddenly everyone is much more interested in giving good service, looking after clients and finding ways to improve bottom-lines. Suddenly, everyone feels like it's their business, too!

Pay more and you will get more, but measure it!

---

*One of the smartest things we ever did was to reward our staff properly.*

---

# 5

# ... BUT IT'S ALSO
# JUST ABOUT YOU

RULE

KNOW WHAT YOU'LL
BE FAMOUS FOR

We've discussed a lot of the 'for the business' stuff already, but there's more to success than just corporate acumen. There are many things that I have first rejected, and then accepted, and seen the benefits of. And others seem to see the same results. I wouldn't be doing this book, or you, the reader, justice if I didn't share them with you. They may seem like the softer elements, but that doesn't make them any less valuable.

# RULE
## 58 KNOW WHAT YOU'LL BE FAMOUS FOR

### BY PAUL BULPITT

*Paul knows the challenge of being an entrepreneur. He co-founded several businesses of his own, including The Wow Company, a specialist, non-traditional accounting firm that serves entrepreneurs exclusively. He was once even the Head of Accounting at Xero. This guy gets the concept of partnerships like few others. He is a great friend and always on speed dial for a coffee when I land in the UK.*

What are you going to be famous for?

Starting, growing and running a business is all-consuming. It eats your time, your focus, your brainpower and almost every waking thought. We spend most of our time with our heads down, caught up in the daily hustle: caring for customers, outsmarting the competition, hiring and developing our team, and improving processes. But when you eventually look up, will you find yourself surprised (or shocked) at where you are headed? Chances are you'll have a plan, but is there a way to increase your chances of success, and get the most value out from the hard work you're pouring in, so you can end up where you actually want to be?

In my experience, those entrepreneurs who have thought about and are absolutely clear on what they want their business to be famous for are the ones who tend to outperform and outlast others. It makes sense. You can't be amazing at everything, so rather than trying – and failing – to be all things to all people, be great at one single thing above all others. Focus. Think carefully. 'What do I want to be famous for?'

You don't need to become famous for the obvious thing. For example, Zappos, the online shoe store, didn't want to be famous for selling shoes; they wanted to be famous for their customer service. So, instead of trying to compete with thousands to be the world's best shoe-sellers, which would have been tough, they chose to compete on customer service within the shoe market, which was easier (for them). And they won, selling millions of shoes in the process.

So, again I ask, 'What is the thing that *you* should be famous for?' Working out the answer can be fun. Imagine a future where people are writing articles and books about your business – what are they writing about, and what headline do they use at the top? Find something you think you (and your team) are uniquely placed to become famous for. Find something you believe will make you a world-beater.

Once you've identified what your core purpose is, the next step is to work out how you can become crazily, absurdly, ridiculously famous for that thing. What would that look like?

When focus meets execution you'll be surprised how quickly your fame builds. With fame will come new customers as your current customers now have something to shout about you. People will want to work with you. People will want to work for you. People will be hammering at your door. As Socrates said, 'Fame is the perfume of heroic deeds'. Go be heroic!

# RULE
## 59 BE AN EARLY BIRD

There is something magical about the first few hours of the day, a time when everything is quiet, there are no disturbances, no ringing phones, no nagging staff – just a time to do whatever you want to. It's a time to tick something off your to-do list and it enables you to start your day with a much better energy than if you wake up and immediately rush to get dressed and go to work, half asleep and half-arsed.

Some call this magic time 4am (most call it 5am). I refer to this 60-minute period as my holy hour because I can do whatever feels right for me. Whether it is to be still and to meditate or write in your journal, whether you use it for training or to do your most important tasks of the day, the overall effect will be to start your day with a win. A calm and positive win.

Many claim that they are not 'morning people' and refuse even to try. Like anything else in life, the longer you do it (or try to do it), the easier it gets and, before you know it, it has become a part of your daily routine.

If you're new to this, or one of those 'nothing happens before my fifth coffee' people, you may need a bit of help to get started. Try to leave your wake-up alarm in another room and then refuse to go back to bed after it's turned off. Or wash your face immediately after getting up. It also helps to drink a glass of water after waking up because your body has been resting for a long period and is dehydrated.

After doing this for a couple of days or weeks, you will realise the true power of this holy hour. It is a time when you can really reflect on your day or solve complicated business problems. Don't waste this special energy and time by doing mundane tasks such as reading, cleaning, replying to emails or being on social media.

It is a magical time, use it as such.

---

*This 60-minute period is my holy hour because I can do whatever feels right for me.*

---

# RULE
## 60      MEDITATION

Wait and hear me out before you skip to the next rule. This is one of the topics I always politely turned away from when I heard it being discussed. After all, I threw out my tie-dye over a decade ago.

Meditation is often something we Westerners don't want to talk about. We think it is some sort of religious technique, borrowed from the East, but meditation is much more than that, and there's science behind it. There are more than 3,000 studies that show the great effects meditation can offer us all, but, more especially, entrepreneurs and business people.

Your focus will increase. You'll be more aware. You will be calmer. Meditation concentrates your grey matter (quite literally).

There are different kinds of meditation and different techniques, but it boils down to this: a dedicated time of focus or contemplation, just quieting the mind, and being mindful.

We live in a world where our minds are constantly jumping from one thought to another without ever being really mindful of what these thoughts actually are, or giving them the attention they deserve. Meditation gives you the ability to let these thoughts pass in a more orderly fashion, so you don't miss out on any potentially life-altering insights.

The research on mindfulness suggests that meditation sharpens skills like attention, memory and emotional intelligence. Meditation builds resilience. It has the potential to decrease anxiety, thereby potentially boosting resilience and performance under stress – all things great entrepreneurs need more of.

Imagine how differently you might handle a situation if you sat still for 20 minutes prior to having to deal with it. And that is what meditation will do over time. It will train your mind to be quieter and because your reactions are more thoughtful, your world will change.

Mindfulness is fast becoming a billion-dollar industry and there is a good reason why. If you are not already meditating, it might be time to try it out. Millions of Buddhists, CEOs, ninjas and entrepreneurs can't be *completely* wrong.

---

*Mindfulness is fast becoming a billion-dollar industry.*

---

# RULE
## 61 START A JOURNAL

*'A life worth living is a life worth recording.'*
— Jim Rohn

A journal is not a diary. It is not a scrapbook. And you don't have to be a teenage girl to get value from one. As entrepreneurs, we are often so busy moving at the speed of light that we seldom stop and just reflect on what is really happening around us. Writing a daily journal is a great routine to combat this. It makes events in our lives trackable, and as soon as we commit them to paper we've marked them as a part of a history we can later reflect on and learn from.

And it also has other benefits. By physically writing your thoughts down, you engage in a creative process that allows you to brainstorm effective solutions and to explore new lines of thinking.

Your journal will also be your private timeline. We often forget where we were, what we were thinking, where our businesses were going. Going back to a journal is a great reminder of how far we have come and a document of the lives we have lived.

A journal may take different forms for different people but the following four questions are a great starting guideline, and a good way to get you started. Every morning ask yourself:

1. What was something great about yesterday?
2. What was something that could have been improved yesterday?
3. What is something that you are grateful for today?
4. What would make today great?

Journaling should not be an unpleasant exercise but rather a fun activity that is part of your day. Journaling the answers to the above four questions on a regular basis will provide you with the necessary reflection and planning needed to make better future decisions as an entrepreneur.

No matter whether you write down your reflections and thoughts on paper or screen, the action of putting words to your thoughts opens up a door that provides insight and clarity in a way that few other exercises can. It is exactly these insights that empower many successful entrepreneurs to rise to the top.

---

*By physically writing your thoughts down, you engage in a creative process.*

---

# RULE
## 62 DON'T SLEEP ONLY WHEN YOU'RE DEAD

The value placed on sleep has plummeted in recent years, as entrepreneurs have continued to brag about how many hours they've clocked versus how many hours of sleep they've lost. We always talk about the hustle and the hard work, yet we don't often talk about what we're losing out on. And the metrics are easy: the less we sleep, the less we hustle and the harder work becomes.

Entrepreneurs need to be productive, and to be productive you need to get rest. Most do not. You spend your days trying to get things done and there is never enough time. Business won't ever be your second priority and therefore sleep is. The ironic thing is that because sleep is not a priority, the business will suffer.

Sleep is a huge issue and the lack thereof can have some pretty negative consequences on your health – from weight gain and getting sick more often to sexual dysfunction and even early death (when you sleep your body produces substances like cytokines, which keep you healthy and infection-free). An unhealthy person can never be a great entrepreneur.

A lack of shut-eye will also have a pronounced effect on your productivity as a business person. When you're tired your brain's synapses pull apart, making thoughts slow and muddy. When your brain is stressed, it makes poor decisions. Cognition will decrease, irritability and irrationality will increase. Creativity will be almost at zero.

If you want to be as productive as possible, you need to 'wake up' to the importance of getting enough sleep. How many hours should you be aiming for? Tons of research has been done on this subject and the range always comes out as between seven and nine hours a night. You can use that as a guideline but, more importantly, listen to your own body. It will tell you when it is tired and needs more sleep.

It became the norm for entrepreneurs to cut down on their sleeping hours, increasing their caffeine intake to compensate. Somehow we came to believe that was the way it had to be if you wanted to create a successful business. But the opposite is true: better sleep will make it easier for you to deal with the challenges involved in entrepreneurship.

Do yourself and your business *and* your staff a favour and get some sleep. What you lose in working hours you'll make up for with an *effective, useful* working *life*.

---

*The less we sleep, the less we hustle and the harder work becomes.*

---

# RULE
## 63

# HEALTHY BODY, HEALTHY BUSINESS

This is a controversial subject for the entrepreneur. We all know that we need to exercise and eat well. But entrepreneurs often claim to be too busy 'for all that stuff'. Early (and late) meetings block our trips to the gym, as do reports, staff meetings and networking sessions. And it's far easier to order a pizza (again) to stave off the barking dogs of hunger while we're stuck late at the office (again).

Your body is the vehicle for your brain. Your brain is the engine of your business. If your body is covered in rust, pulling apart at the seams, leaking oil and generally shutting down, how long until your brain and business follow suit? To further extend the metaphor, if it is accurate, why would you dump carcinogenic, poisonous junk in your fuel tank?

Humans have evolved to be mobile. But working people spend upwards of 60 per cent of every day on their asses, frozen and staring at their devices, tapping away on their laptops like fat tyrannosaurs. Another 30 per cent of the day is spent on their backs. Our body atrophies, along with our minds.

Much like sleep and meditation, exercise reduces stress and anxiety. It allows your system to perform at its peak, which means your mind is far more effective. Exercise releases endorphins, which make you more positive and happy. Good, decent, healthy food has similar effects. And you won't be pushing your health insurance premiums through the ceiling.

There's also a more superficial reason to exercise. If you're not in shape (or at least not in a pleasant one) you're perceived as being less effective and less dedicated, whether that is true or not.

Don't pay later for something that you could take care of now. Where is the sense in working your life away, becoming overstressed and burning out, just to have enough money one day to pay for your health care and to try to get your health back – success now; health later. It is a common scenario among entrepreneurs, but it is simply not an option for the smart one.

Getting as physical as Olivia Newton-John isn't necessary, but a little movement on a regular basis will only do good things for you. By sacrificing a few hours a week to a run, climb or swim you will change your whole working life. Start being more conscious of what you do and make a commitment to yourself to move around at least once a day. Just once. Get your heart rate up and sweat a little. Eat good food. Sleep well.

If Sir Richard Branson can make time to kite-surf, you can squeeze in a few hours at the gym. And he claims that exercise gives him an extra four hours of productivity every day. Check out Timothy Ferriss' book *The 4-Hour Body* if you really want to get serious.

Again, it is not the destination, it's the journey – make it count.

---

*If Sir Richard Branson can make time to kite-surf, you can squeeze in a few hours at the gym.*

---

# RULE 64

# AN EVENING ROUTINE

Many people are pretty productive in the morning and have a great routine to match. Early risers seem to get more done and live happier lives (see the earlier rule). They meditate, have a proper breakfast, do some training and the day starts well. But it can end in many different ways. It might be good, it might be bad, but it is *never* consistent. A morning routine is only the first *half* of a productive day – the other is the evening routine that precedes it. Yes, you read that correctly: the previous evening sets up the following day.

An evening is often just an open loop at the end of the day. Many have nothing specific to do, and it might therefore end up being used for late nights at the office, late wasted nights in front of the TV or an unproductive late afternoon on social media. What a waste of precious time …

It is a great advantage for entrepreneurs to have an evening routine and manage it the same way as they do the morning routine. But to keep to the routine, and its benefits, you need to set up some structures. Go home at a particular time, have dinner with your family (with cellphones off). Set aside 30 minutes to read a biography. Spend an hour playing with the dogs. 9pm-10pm can be used to research trends. Do whatever works for you but do it consistently and you will soon find that you get a lot more done.

Setting guidelines for yourself for the evenings will keep you responsible and conscious of how you spend this time.

It will make you more productive but, even more importantly, it will determine how the next day goes. What you do each night can ensure your success the following day. Go to bed late and you will be tired. Eat unhealthy food and you will feel the effects the next day.

If you are looking to staying focused and conquering more today, start by fixing the *night before*.

---

*An evening routine will make you more productive but, even more importantly, it will determine how the next day goes.*

---

# RULE
## 65    SET SOME LIMITS

This rule could have been called 'A work/life balance' but you would have skipped right over it. Balance is only possible if you have a 9-5 life as an employee. As an entrepreneur? Not so much. Entrepreneurs have to *force* it.

You will *live* your business. It will be the first thing you think about when you wake up in the morning and it will be your last thought when you go to bed at night. Or at least it will be like that for most entrepreneurs. Your life will be different from most of those around you which means you can't use them as a point of reference when it comes to seeing what balance looks like.

Having morning and evening routines will help you to start adding meaningful, non-work elements to your already cluttered life, making it a more precious one, but we need to be realistic about what is required and what can be achieved.

I know many entrepreneurs who tried to achieve this balance by adhering to strict rules. They wouldn't sort out personal issues between 08h00 and 17h00 and they would never answer a business call over a weekend or at night. This is cool, but it will most likely just freak you out in the end, as it did them ... You can try to avoid the work call on a Saturday but you will end up stressing about it for the entire weekend. It's better just to take the call and deal with it.

There is a different approach: Make peace with what you need to deal with and work around that. Take work calls, within reason, over the weekend, but also don't make

156                                90 RULES FOR ENTREPRENEURS

an issue about having to drop your kid off at school on a Monday morning.

Once you implement basic rules – such as not working from home or making calls or checking email at night – just relax and give attention to the few things that will come up and need your attention. 90 per cent of the things will be within your control anyway.

As an entrepreneur, you have an opportunity to live life according to your own rules. Don't spoil it by letting your life be driven by inflexible rules you've set yourself. Work is your life and life is your work. Just find a way to let the two work in harmony.

---

*Your life will be different from most of those around you which means you can't use them as a point of reference.*

---

# RULE
## 66

# THE 90-MINUTE RULE

Whether you've just started your business or it has been going for years, the one thing entrepreneurs always need more of is *time*. In fact, that has been a fairly thick theme throughout this section. But what about managing your *at work time*?

Business owners have it bad, because they have time-eaters from two sides. First, everyone is trying to connect with you for something: to work for you, to work *with* you, to get your business. And on the other side, because entrepreneurs always see the opportunity in everything, we want to solve everything. We thus run the risk of getting involved in too many projects – spreading ourselves too thin – and consequently neglect the things that are truly important. Where does it all go …?

Over the years, I've tried many techniques to maximise my time and there is one that stands out. I call it the 90-minute rule because, well, that's all it is. But it's paid off.

Use the first 90 minutes of your day to work on the ONE thing that is most important to you – the one thing your business needs, the one thing that will make the biggest difference in your business. Schedule those 90 minutes in your diary and treat them as a meeting with the most important person on earth. Switch off your phone, lock yourself in a room and just work on that one thing. Ninety minutes may seem like nothing, but over time it adds up and makes a massive difference.

We all know business owners need to work more ON their businesses rather than IN their businesses. The 90-minute rule will give you that opportunity, without throwing too much else out.

---

*Use the first 90 minutes of your day to work on the ONE thing that is most important to you.*

---

# RULE
## 67

# STAY TRUE TO YOURSELF

I once read that Mark Lamberti, the founder of Massmart Holdings (Builders Warehouse, etc) wrote a letter to himself about the person that he strives to be one day. That was back in the early days, before he achieved much of anything.

He carried this letter with him all the time. Every day, at random times, he would open it up, read it and compare his own actions against the person he said he wanted to be. It kept him grounded and on track.

You see, you can't be a loving husband or a great dad if you treat other people badly. You can't be a great entrepreneur or a great boss if you are always complaining and not doing the things great leaders do. But we forget these things in the midst of battle and, before we know it, we're not who we once were – and we're not happy about the contrast.

We may strive to be a certain type of person, but personal growth happens over decades – how do you make sure you are staying true to who you *want to be*, when the changes happen so slowly? I thought Mark's letter was an excellent way of reminding himself *about himself* in the midst of crazy, everyday life.

Mark went further and made copies of the letter and gave them to the people closest to him and asked them to help him out by telling him when he was not acting the way his ideal person would.

Our seconds become our hours, our hours become our days and our days are our life. Before you know it, years have gone, and you've drifted off course. It is impossible to create the perfect life without taking those perfect actions each and every single day.

As an entrepreneur, family man, friend, parent, I dare you to write this letter to yourself, to keep it with you and constantly remind yourself who you want to be, what you want to have, and be conscious of how that person would live *their* seconds.

---

*You can't be a great boss if you are always complaining and not doing the things great leaders do.*

---

# RULE
## 68

# ON BEING VISIONARY

## BY VINNY LINGHAM

*Vinny is yet another person I was fortunate enough to meet on* Shark Tank South Africa. *His mind is 100 per cent entrepreneurial, and all he thinks about, all the time, is the 'next deal'. You can see him as an angel, or as a threat, and many do, but you cannot deny his successes. He has founded and run companies like Civic, Gyft and Yola, Inc, and is also the co-founder of Silicon Cape, which will do to South Africa what San Francisco did for the States.*

To be a visionary founder you have got to see ahead, you have got to see around corners, you have got to believe in things that no one else really believes in. When you start a company you will have a very clear, long-term vision for your startup, but don't be surprised that most people around you, be it friends, family and peers, will not see it, or understand it. Do not let anyone else's doubts derail you.

When you ask someone what a graph that shows success looks like, most times they will draw an imaginary line with their finger that goes steadily and steeply up to the right. In reality, the line goes up and down, with lots of squiggles in between. Entrepreneurship is very much like this. There will be ebbs and flows, bad days and good days.

In the startup periods of all the companies that I have built there have been moments when I thought 'this is going to crash badly' or 'we are a day away from closing down'. Every company gets to a point where you think you are going to fail, but you need to keep plugging away – that's just startup life.

A trait that all entrepreneurs need is perseverance. It takes blood, sweat and tears in those early years. Know that your returns, at first, will not always be reflective of your efforts.

I worked seven days a week for many years. There are no short cuts when learning a new business or industry – you need to work harder and longer hours than anyone else to get ahead. Get used to 18-hour days, six to seven days a week; that's what it takes. And hard work is not enough, you need to be smart, savvy and have tons of perseverance. If it were easy, everyone would be doing it.

If you have a fear of failure you shouldn't start a business. How are you going to try things if you are too scared? It's OK to fail, as long as you learn a lesson from it (and never repeat it). The whole point of the startup is to run a series of experiments of which 90 per cent may, and probably will, fail. But the experiments that do thrive will allow you to get real market insights and you can build something really successful out of them. In all the companies that I have started we have run tests, tests and more tests, asking many questions like 'what about this?' and 'what about that?', 'do the customers want this or do they want that?'

Persevere, take risks, question everything, work smart, surround yourself with clever people – it gets easier as you go along, and the journey to success is worth all of the worries and fears.

# RULE
## 69

# THE GOOD GUY
# ALWAYS WINS

Isn't that the complete opposite of what we've always been told? I remember that when I was a kid, money was seen as an evil thing and people who had money were either stealing it or were taking advantage of other people or abusing the system to enrich themselves. I was taught that the business world was a cruel place and that you would never win by being a good guy. Movies like *Wall Street* (remember the Gordon Gekko line, 'Greed is good'?) didn't exactly help, either.

But my experience in the business world has shown me something completely different. I've realised that, in the long run, it is the good guy who always wins. The good guys are the entrepreneurs who build the really great businesses. People love working with them, they attract good staff who are loyal to them, and who work harder for them, suppliers give them better deals and contracts, and they go home content with themselves, to a family who respect and love them. They are trusted when others are feared. The world always roots for the good guy.

Yes, you often see guys who are enriching themselves by cheating the system or being unethical in their businesses. But in the long run those guys are seldom successful or happy. Their staff leave and bad-mouth them to others. Their clients dry up. Their friends find better ones. Banks shut their vaults. Networks close down. Somewhere in the future their actions will catch up with them and they will lose everything and waste away, alone, on their deathbeds, regretting their entire lifetime.

This is far more true today than it was in previous years. This isn't the 80s any more. We are moving more and more into a world where social media posts spread like wildfire and the bad guys are exposed to a much wider audience than before. You can't hide your actions. And this power has made us far less tolerant of 'evil' (whatever you see that as) men. Just look at the Dakota oil-line protests, the Occupy movement, anti-Zuma marches and pretty much everything that Edward Snowden and Anonymous are fighting against.

The world tells us that the 'nice guys finish last', but in most cases the nice entrepreneurs are the more successful ones and, even if they are not, they are definitely the happiest ones.

There is enough wrong with the world without your adding to it. And you have the power to do so much the right way and actually benefit from it.

---

*The world always roots for the good guy.*

---

# RULE 70

# LISTEN TO THAT NAGGING LITTLE VOICE

When big problems blow up entrepreneurs face super-massive challenges. But many big problems start out as much smaller ones. They come in many forms: an employee is caught defrauding the company, someone is badly injured on duty, or a rude email loses you your biggest client – the list is endless.

More often than not these really big events don't occur out of the blue, but were things that were waiting to get adult enough to happen. And you probably *knew* they were there, gestating quietly in the corner. But you brushed them off and dealt with the things that were right there in your face. The important stuff. Or you ignored them because they made you feel a little too uncomfortable. The result is the same.

You *saw* that the employee was driving a new car and living beyond his means. You *knew* your safety codes were out of date, and you had an *inkling* that your big client had been dissatisfied for some time. You're aware of many things in your business. Pay attention to that little voice of yours, listen to it, and deal with the problems before they go atomic. When you feel something is not right, fix it immediately. It will take less time and might save you a lot of money, or even save your business.

Your gut feeling is your secret weapon to success and trusting it will help you in the workplace and beyond. But you need to listen to it. And then act on it.

*Deal with the problems before they go atomic.*

# 6

# THE MASTER
# OF YOUR
# ENVIRONMENT

If you want to grow, you need to plant yourself in the right soil. This is the environment you create and immerse yourself in, as well as the people who are there to support you, teach you and nurture you. It's your environment, and you need to be the master of it. Control the environment around you, and you will control your life.

# RULE
## 71

# NO BUSINESS IS AN ISLAND

A successful business is dependent on the entrepreneur behind it but, more importantly, the relationships that the entrepreneur has with others. Everyone says that networking is important, but it's about more than just networking. It's about building relationships with suppliers, clients, staff, everyone. It's about working as a collective, where the success of each separate entity strengthens the success of the group. It's about win-win-win.

It is often the entrepreneur with good relationships who will get the deal. People work with people they genuinely like and relate to. Suppliers will bend over backwards for people who have done them favours in the past. Your customers might find it easy enough to find another supplier, but breaking up a good relationship will be much more difficult, especially because of all the extra work you've put in because you act like you are (and you *are*) on their team. Your network will refer you and do your marketing for you, as you will do for them. They'll enlighten you to new trends in your industry. You start to share credibility. This is group strength.

Every successful entrepreneur will tell you that their most important asset is their network (and they don't usually mean social network) – the people they actually know and work with in real time because they're the ones who actually get things done. One real, solid relationship in the real world is worth more than 10,000 social media links, likes or followers.

Spend your time building quality relationships – with everyone – and you will soon find business a whole lot easier.

You'll get by with a little help from your friends.

---

*It's about win-win-win.*

---

# RULE 72

# THE BIGGER THEY ARE ...

## BY ADRIAAN VAN DER SPUY

*Adriaan was one of the contestants on* Shark Tank South Africa *in one of the most emotional episodes to date. He and his uncle found a funding partner in Romeo, and then subsequently Adriaan started a completely new sporting goods import business, which he asked me to invest in. He grew that company to seven-figure-size in very short time and it is now the sole distributor of one of the biggest sporting goods brands on the planet. I liked everything about how he runs things, so I pulled him over to run our VC fund, which he now does as my partner. He's a great people person and proof that an amazing salesman can build any kind of business.*

'The bigger they come, the harder they fall ...' are the lyrics that Jimmy Cliff sang. I cannot remember when I first heard it, but I absolutely loved it, and that one sentence still resonates with me on a daily basis.

But nobody really discusses the ugly flipside of this which is, '*the bigger they come, the harder they hit!*'

As entrepreneurs we all face behemoths and massive obstacles on our way to reaching our goals and dreams. It could be a giant sales target in front of you, or maybe a large competitor cutting costs (because they can afford to) and forcing you to do the same. What is so critically important is how we deal with these situations. There can only be one of two outcomes: either *they* fall hard, or they hit hard, or *you* do.

In my personal experience the only time that we allow these things to beat us is when we give up, and the only time we give up is when we lose the 'strong and barely controllable emotion' that most of us refer to as *passion*.

When Francois and I started our import business, Oltre Global, to bring in (mainly) gymnastics equipment, I didn't really have a major vision or a super dream for the company. We didn't have the accounting or the business skills. We didn't have storage facilities. And we most definitely didn't have money. We placed an order with an overseas supplier, with whom I had dealt with in the past, and waited for it to arrive. 'Between six and eight weeks,' the supplier promised, and it was the longest six weeks of my life. The excitement was huge and we couldn't stop talking about it (I think my family thought I was going crazy). All we could talk was gymnastics, and sales, and potential margins and then all of it all over again. We didn't know for sure that we would sell anything but we knew we would try, and everyone around us knew that – and the entire order was sold before it reached our sunny shores.

So we doubled our next order. I mean, if history is a decent teacher, what could go wrong? Then we received an email from our forwarding company that Customs had decided to stop our container. 'Out of hundreds that come in every day, they decide to stop *our* container?' I yelled at our forwarding agent. 'How is that even possible?'

Our company was but a few months old and the first major obstacle was staring us in the face. And it was a doozy. We had a very tight budget and every cost was calculated to the last cent. The extra fees amounted to around £1,000 on top of the quoted amount, our margins were shot and I remember wondering if it was worth all the trouble. But we hit back, and we survived.

It's not such a big deal for us now, but it was gargantuan back then. As I am writing this today we still have a million miles to go in this company but I can look back at that defining moment and say that if we didn't love what we were doing so much, we might have called it quits right there.

Often it's passion that is the stone that will fell your Goliath. Passion needs to be created and recreated daily. Remind yourself why you are doing what you are doing. Look back on the successes, and the failures, and allow them to stir passion for things to come. Get excited about the little things. Surround yourself with passionate individuals who can ignite the passion in you and then let the behemoths drop around you, one by one.

# RULE

## 73 UNCOUPLE YOUR BUSINESS AND PERSONAL AFFAIRS

Small businesses are usually run by one owner and it often happens that this owner lives from the business account. School fees are paid from it, groceries are purchased with it and the house is right on there too.

There are a few reasons why you should separate your business and personal affairs:

- *Budget*: You can't budget properly for your business if it is too mixed up with your personal expenses. It's too messy. Since most entrepreneurs don't always understand their business's cash flow cycles, they may use money for personal expenses only to find that they can't pay bills when the business cash flow takes a dip.

- *Legal*: If you don't separate your business and personal affairs, then creditors (or anyone else with a claim against you) can claim that your business is not really a separate entity and courts may rule that you are not protected by the company's structure and you will be held personally liable for any company debt.

- *Selling the business:* If you ever decide to sell your business, it will be very difficult to split personal expenses from business expenses and potential buyers may be put off when they see the business financials in such a state.

The best advice for any entrepreneur is to separate business and personal matters right from the start. Pay yourself a salary and keep to your personal budget. This will enable you to run a much better business without all the personal clutter.

*Separate business and personal matters right from the start.*

# RULE
## 74

# TRUST, BUT DON'T BE STUPID

Everyone has been disappointed at some time in their lives, and often by the people you least expected it from. Trust is not given, it is earned. But even after being earned, don't be naive about it. Temper that trust with a splash of cynicism regarding the human race.

There are many entrepreneurs who have lost everything because they placed all their trust in a certain individual or group of people. Accountants and financial directors have stolen millions from entrepreneurs who trusted them with their banking. Sales reps and account managers have made businesses go into liquidation after taking all the customers or key accounts. Business partners who you trusted with your life – the godparents of your children! – left with your business and hard-earned cash, laughing all the way.

Business is a funny thing and money makes people react in unpredictable ways. Business people are still just people. And not all of them are awesome. Service Level Agreements were invented for this very reason.

The smart entrepreneurs protect themselves against these possibilities. As a basic principle, draft and conclude proper agreements with everyone you do business with. Include restraint of trade clauses with employees, partners and suppliers. Set up internal controls in the company to ensure that no one individual is allowed to make payments or have access to cash.

Never rely on customers to fulfil their promises (see RULE 22) and don't take risks that could sink you. Customers often over-promise and under-deliver, so be careful with their credit terms and ensure that there are proper agreements in place in case anything should go wrong.

These are all basic principles in business and most corporates will comply with them but the small business owner wants to hustle and conclude the deal. That's a shaky tightrope to walk when you don't have piles of cash to cushion the fall.

Trust, but don't be stupid about it.

---

*Business people are still just people. And not all of them are awesome.*

---

# RULE
## 75

# ON THE PAGES OF GIANTS

*'If I have seen further it is by standing on
the shoulders of giants.'*

– Sir Isaac Newton

I have met many great people who have played key roles in my life. But only later in my life. I grew up in a poor family in a small town and I did not have anyone to coach me on how to start a business. I'm partly glad about this, because it taught me the biggest lesson about mentorship: that you can find it in books. Books are extensions of the people who write them and, if you can't find those people in a coffee shop, you can still draw on their insights in a book store.

I read every book written by every great entrepreneur – especially autobiographies. This gave me a glimpse into their lives, the essence of what they believed in, and I learned from, and was inspired by, these people.

I often hear people saying that you could ask anyone to mentor you and they will most likely be willing to do so. Rubbish. The most successful people I know hardly have time to see their own families and those are the people who we really need to learn from. They might not have the time to have coffee with you but they share so many ideas and thoughts in interviews and content, that they've almost removed the need for them to be there in person. Choose great giants in your field and consume everything about them. You will learn more than you are capable of taking in.

Nowadays, I have the opportunity to sit with billionaire friends and business partners. It's great learning from them but I learn as much from the many great business books I read and the interviews I watch. Mentorship is all around you, but it's cellulose-bound, podcasted, blogged or streaming on CNBC.

*Choose great giants in your field and consume everything about them.*

# RULE
## 76  YOU ARE WHAT YOU EAT

Your success is probably more dependent on those you have around you than on your own abilities. Harsh, but honest. I'm not talking about friends or partners here; I'm talking about the people who *get it*. You cannot be a jack-of-all-trades, which means you're going to rely on those in your vicinity to prop you up when you need them to.

The most successful entrepreneurs always surround themselves with a trusted adviser (usually an accountant, a lawyer or a broker), a financial institution and peers.

Your peers are those on your level – not just guys you can have a beer with. Jim Rohn famously said that you will be the average of the five people you spend the most time with, and it couldn't be truer for the entrepreneur. You need business-minded friends, fellow entrepreneurs, who understand the journey of entrepreneurship and who can support and encourage you. The average person will always see the downside to everything and that's not what you need. The journey of being an entrepreneur is a difficult one and your biggest support will come from those who are in the same boat as you are, have insights to share, and understand what you're going through. Surround yourself with people who are better than you so that you, in turn, can be better.

Who do you spend the most time with? Are they giants?

These entities you surround yourself with should also have the skills and access you don't. When you start out, and more especially when you begin to grow, you need a 'financial institution' – not necessarily a bank – that understands you and your business and can help you with financing. It is so important to build a real relationship with someone in that space who can help you when times are tough or when you need to grow.

Big banks seldom support small businesses and there are several alternative finance options available for small business owners. The key is to start these relationships early, when you don't need them, so that, when you do, the trust is already there.

The journey of an entrepreneur is often a lonely one; you can try to do everything yourself but it will be a long and tough road. You need people to have your back, and you need them to be there when they are most needed. I was lucky enough to have some of the greatest entrepreneurs in my corner, and to call them friends, and it's they who I blame for my success.

*Who do you spend the most time with?*
*Are they giants?*

# RULE
## 77

# THE SECRET TO ANYTHING: FIND THE RECIPE

It's easy to make a loaf of bread; you find the recipe, you find the ingredients, you execute the instructions and bang it in the oven. Simple. Can we apply the same logic in business or anywhere else? Yes. You find the recipe and you execute it. It might not be in a book with detailed instructions, but with a little help you can find out pretty much how to do anything, including building a business. Whatever you're trying to do – implement a new policy, train staff better, or get into a new market – many have done it before you, so why should you figure out everything for yourself? Not everyone needs to be a chef!

Whenever you want to achieve something, talk to people who have done it, read books about it, then replicate it – bang it in the oven. You want a great new body? Find someone who has the recipe figured out. You find the recipe, the plan, you execute it and the results almost always are a given.

To be successful in any industry, you need to be a specialist. What makes one a specialist? Knowing more than 99 per cent of other people. And how do you achieve that? By reading five books on a specific topic. Yes, by reading five books you will have done something that 99 per cent of others haven't. Specialist. Easy. You've got the recipe. That's what I've done with the book you're holding right now; it's a recipe book.

It is said that knowledge is power, but *applied* knowledge is the power to achieve anything. We live in a world where information is literally in the palm of our hand. We can find out anything in seconds. Yet we make a big deal about not knowing how to do certain things.

People always tend to look for an easier way to accomplish something, and finding the right recipe *is that easy way*. And, when you 'bang it in the oven', you've moved a lot closer to your goal and a lot faster than the original chef ever did.

---

## *Not everyone needs to be a chef!*

---

# RULE
## 78 DECLUTTER

As a business leader you will use systems to grow a great business. But, over time, many of these systems are built upon, changed and tweaked, and then new ones are added. This is true of all the parts of your business – they accumulate rubbish, junk and legacy. These get in the way, much like all the 'must-have' tools in your garage that you constantly trip over. You need to make it as easy as possible for your team to perform their tasks by removing all the clutter.

There are many tasks and procedures in companies that are carried out without any reason whatsoever. Most of them are done because that's the way it has always been and no one is questioning why.

Clutter works like the accumulated gunk in your engine – it makes everything run less efficiently, and the effect is compounded over time. A company gets its staff to complete timesheets on a daily basis; they spend hours every month doing them and, in the end, no one looks at them. This is a waste of sellable resources. Security guards who sign in visitors, give them a form to complete, don't look at it but allow the visitor in anyway, are wasting clients' time. What's the point of these processes if they are clearly useless and time-wasting? They are redirecting energy away from where it should be spent.

As business owners and leaders you need to look at all your systems and processes and ask yourself if they are really valid or simply a waste of time. What do you really want to achieve with them and are they worth the time spent on them – do they pay off? Question all your systems constantly, lest they become the red tape that binds you into immobility.

And when you are left with valid processes and systems, how can you further automate them to give even more time to your employees? If you ever get to the point where you don't want to make things easier (because then you won't know what to do with your employees), you are in the wrong game.

Great entrepreneurs will simplify and automate as far as possible, as often as possible, and will either retrench staff or use them elsewhere more effectively. Don't let being 'uselessly complicated' be what gunks up your engine, sucks your profits, and erodes what you've built.

---

*Question all your systems constantly.*

---

# 7

# BE CAREFUL WHO YOU GET IN THE POOL WITH ...

# RULE
## 79

# BEWARE OF FUNDING

Or rather, you *shouldn't* need funding – at least not at the start of your venture, and hopefully not halfway through the journey either. By getting financially involved with someone – human or institutional – you're essentially opening a door for them.

This may be a good thing, and it may be necessary, but it's always risky. You've become beholden to an entity that may, but probably won't, have your best interests at heart.

Banks are looking for a sustainable return on their investment. It's unlikely they'll give you money anyway but, if they do, don't believe their marketing campaigns. They're not there to support you, or to help you grow. They're there to make money *off* you in repayments and interest, and will charge and act accordingly.

Investors have similar motives, but they can often be even more involved in the day-to-day operational side. They'll make decisions and take actions that will often be of benefit, but their motivations, too, are self-guided. So, they're not thinking about your dream, or your staff, nearly as much as you are; they're thinking about their own financial success *through* you. (More on this in the next rule.)

There may be times when a cash injection is the only option for future growth. I'm not saying avoid it at all costs, but do the best you can to be self-reliant. There's a reason the phrase 'neither a borrower nor a lender be' is still used today. If you do need to get another party involved, be very, very careful who you choose. They may fund you, but there may be another 'f' word they do to you, too …

---

*Don't believe banks' marketing campaigns.*

---

# RULE
## 80

# DON'T GIVE UP EQUITY

This is so important that I have written another rule about it. *Whatever you do, don't give up equity.* Try every avenue possible before even thinking of it. You will often hear people say 'equity is the most expensive form of finance', and they are right. We'll go through it in this rule and hopefully the outcome will convince you never to do it.

New entrepreneurs are often eager to give up equity for cash. When you start a business, it is worth nothing so giving up equity is not a big deal. But when the business grows and its value becomes substantial, then equity is the biggest deal ever.

You know the three basic methods of funding: by getting a loan, by giving up equity or by yourself.

When taking out a loan, you will pay interest on it, but once it is paid, the loan is history and you are still the only owner.

Giving up equity, on the other hand, will be a very costly exercise in the long run. One day when you sell whatever the business is valued at will be divided between the shareholders in relation to their equity percentage and, depending on the percentage, this may be a huge chunk. On top of that, equity holders would earn a percentage of the yearly profits of the company (in the form of dividends). When this is all added up, and provided that you have built a good profitable company, it will be much, much more than interest on a loan will ever be. And, these guys have a right to make decisions about your business and how it's run! *Your* business!

Also take note that nowadays most private investors will fund a business, take equity, but also expect the amount to be repaid as if it were a loan. Ouch.

When you fund a business yourself, it might be a slower process, but the business will be 100 per cent yours. And if you decide to sell it one day the proceeds will all come to you – 100 per cent return on your hard work.

Entrepreneurs might decide to take up such offers, reasoning that the funds will enable them to start a business and, without it, they would never be able to get out of the garage. That's fine, but first look at all available options and understand the implications of giving up equity.

---

*Equity will be a very costly exercise in the long run.*

---

# RULE
## 81    HOW TO PITCH

There is far too much emphasis placed on the lack of funding and too little on hustling day and night – of being creative in finding funds and doing whatever it takes. By now, you know that funding should be your last option. But if it is something you really cannot manage without, and you've thought through the risks, then we need to talk about how to do it.

Contrary to popular belief, there is a lot of cash in our economy waiting to be used on great entrepreneurs and businesses. But, sadly, there are not many great entrepreneurs with profitable businesses ready to be funded, which makes investors very picky. There's a massive pool of people wanting investment, and that makes it difficult to see the wood for the trees. So, if you are 'one of the good ones', you need to get your story straight and make sure that they see that.

Being on *Shark Tank* showed me exactly how fraught with issues the pitching process really is. Entrepreneurs are often selling things that investors aren't buying.

Where do you start? With the basics. Prepare properly. Know what you want and why you want it. Know what you will do with the money and how you will repay it. To the cent. Make sure you know what they will be getting in return for it, and sell that even harder (*that's* what they're buying). You need to have a proper plan in place and you need to be able to convince investors that they will get their return. 40 per cent of the pitch will be around numbers – so make sure you know them. 40 per cent will be about your product – live it. The rest you can wing with confidence and knowledge of yourself and your business. Don't waffle – get to the point. Don't obfuscate – you'll be caught out.

Lastly, don't see investors as superior to you. If it's right, it will be a partnership. You are entitled to ask questions of them and ensure that they are the right fit. Because you'll be getting more than just their money (see the previous two rules *again*). Ask them what they want out of it and see if it matches what you have on offer. Ask them about other businesses they've been involved in, and how those panned out. See if you like them as people. There's no point getting funding from someone and knowing that it won't work. You will lose a lot of time and your business might never see the light of day.

And if they reject you? Learn from it, even if you don't agree. Go back to the drawing board, amend the plan (if you need to) and get ready for your next pitch. Never give up.

---

*Entrepreneurs are often selling things that investors aren't buying.*

---

# RULE
## 82 DON'T SLEEP WITH
## A STRANGER

Would you marry a stranger? While Russia may have built a fairly substantial mail-order business on the premise that they will, the thought makes most people a little uncomfortable. But new entrepreneurs often enter into a partnership with someone they don't really know. On paper, the person has value, so they register a company, draft an agreement and start doing business. In most cases, these partnerships break apart very early, and the company gets filed in the drawer of 'costly mistakes'. In some cases, the business *does* take off but the relationship still falters and things don't end well – usually in court. It is messy. And even more expensive.

If you're not 100 per cent, absolutely, positively, sure that you know the person, don't bet the farm on them. And you don't have to. A joint venture, for instance, is a less risky way to get the 'on paper' expertise without the ball and chain.

Whenever you want to do something with someone, think of doing it as a JV. Your partner will have their company, they will run it the way they want to. You have your company, and you run it the way you want to. And then you do business together. You draft an agreement and you operate independently, although you work together on certain things.

After you have had time to evaluate the relationship and are able to justify working closer together, you can form a new company and operate as a single entity. By this time, you know and understand your partner and you will have avoided most of the risks involved in starting a business together.

Having said this, never just rely on the relationship and believe that it will always be smooth sailing. Ensure that you draft proper agreements and that both parties are 100 per cent happy with the terms and commitments of such an agreement.

It is an unfortunate fact that most partnerships will blow up, although people never think that at the start. I know of people who were friends for sixty years, then started a business together and the great friendship ended after just a year. Families have broken up because of business deals going wrong. It happens all the time. I have seen partners who leave, taking all the clients with them, and conveniently leaving behind the debt.

To mitigate against this, don't commit to anything formal before testing it out. And when you do commit, ensure that you have everything on paper and that all parties have agreed to the terms.

---

*New entrepreneurs often enter into a partnership with someone they don't really know.*

---

# WHO HAS YOUR BACK?

Friends are very important on your entrepreneurial journey but one relationship is more important than any other: your life partner. Many successful entrepreneurs have attributed their gigantic organisations to their spouses, because of the massive impact that person had on their ability to achieve their goals. Equally, many aspiring entrepreneurs died not realising their dreams because of the lack of support from the one person who was closest to them.

The journey of entrepreneurship is not an easy one. You will need to sacrifice many things, you will have many early mornings and even more late nights. You need a partner, a husband, a wife, who will understand this journey and support you 100 per cent.

Many partners want you to succeed, and enjoy the money and the status that comes with it, but they are not willing to accept the sacrifices that need to be made in order to achieve it. Initially you can try to juggle this relationship with your desire to build a big business, but it won't last. The challenges that you face day to day as an entrepreneur are too extreme to handle if you don't have the support you need.

There can be nothing worse than getting home after a long, hard day at the office and becoming involved in an argument because you have worked late, or being crunched beneath immense stress to finish a project and not be allowed to turn on your computer.

It's still going to be tricky, and there will probably be a few dishes thrown. Circumstances might not always be ideal but your partner needs to be fully aware that this is what it takes to build your dream.

If you have a partner who doesn't understand this, have an honest and open discussion with them. Explain what you are going through and that you are doing it for them as much as for yourself. If they won't try to accommodate you, it is time to choose: your partner or business?

---

*Many entrepreneurs attribute their success to their spouse.*

---

# 84   BANISHING THE MYTH OF BALANCE

## BY DAWN NATHAN-JONES

*Dawn and I have been friends since we both appeared as Sharks on the South African Shark Tank show. But you probably know her as the powerhouse behind the growth and repositioning of Imperial Car Rental (now Europcar). Since stepping down as CEO of this industry giant, Dawn has been involved in many smaller entrepreneurial ventures, which has given her a unique perspective on both the small and large sides of the business world.*

One of the most clichéd business buzz-phrases of the last decade is the one about 'balance'. About how we need to make sure we pay as much attention to our families, relationships and hobbies as we do to our businesses. It's 'work hard, play hard' in a new suit. And often we base our worth as a human being not on how successful we are, but on how perfectly our balance sits. On how good a parent *and* businesswoman we can be, simultaneously. This is one of the most common questions I get asked as a female entrepreneur, especially *by* female entrepreneurs, who are often still struggling under the perceived status quo of gender roles from the 1970s.

As someone who has spent much of her life on the fulcrum between these states I can tell you all, categorically, that this does more harm than good . . .

'Balance' implies an equal distribution of time or effort between the different facets of your life, and it's this that is so damaging. When we try and be everything to everyone, we flitter from pillar to post in a never-ending cycle and end up accomplishing almost nothing of worth. You need to let go of the things that slow you down, so you can maintain your focus on the things that pay the kinds of dividends you're looking for and align with your unique aspirations. To really succeed, you need to have the drive to move constantly forward, which is near impossible if you're always looking over your shoulder to make sure you're not 'unbalancing' the other facets of your life.

Instead, define what balance *means to you*. An entrepreneur needs to dash the guilt they feel about too much time spent at work and not enough time with the family (after all, don't we do the former to benefit the latter?), and do what needs to be done. A mom must often do the opposite and that is just as ok. But, when we stop doing what we think we're supposed to ('balance') we can start being strategic with what we *must* do. When we decide on our own rules, we empower ourselves, and this allows us to make much better choices.

So, find your own balance and, by doing so, start to become the authentic you. This inevitably removes your insecurities and will replace them with a sturdy, unshakable confidence, rooted firmly in that authenticity. The most inspirational people we meet in this life are the ones who live authentically and make intentional decisions.

In the early days, as a female entrepreneur, showing emotions or putting something else on the same level as my career were, to me, signs of weakness. Once I realised how bound by balance I was and untethered myself from it, I found my path and my voice. I made a decision to courageously lead not only with my head, but also with my heart, and to prioritise what was important to me. I was able to step out of EXCO meetings to fetch my son from school. To be a better parent and a better leader. I was able to put my time and effort, in the right measures, into the things I wanted to pay dividends.

I have since learned that defining my own balance was indeed one of my greatest strengths. It is one of yours, too, and, trust me, your family, shareholders, parents, staff, friends and kids will thank you for it.

# 8

# CONSTANT REMINDERS

RULE

DON'T REPLACE
YOUR CUSTOMERS,
GROW THEM

To me this last section is also one of the most important. These are the things you have to continually remind yourself of, as you progress on your journey. They are the few things that will always be true, and things we all constantly forget about. Pop a bookmark or a sticky note in here, and keep coming back.

# RULE
## 85

# DON'T REPLACE YOUR CUSTOMERS; GROW THEM

We've all heard the story that it is much cheaper to look after existing customers than to look for new ones, but for some reason businesses are very bad at doing this. We think acquisition is the metric we should use to judge our growth, instead of retention. If you can get a customer, you've got good marketing. If you can *keep* a customer, you've got a great business.

Most companies run a very smooth sales system. A potential customer makes contact and immediately a salesperson is on the line with them, a sales meeting is scheduled, an agreement is signed, the customer gets invoiced. Then it stops. When the customer has an issue, there is no one to take the call. They request a meeting but it can't be arranged. Customer service is lagging. We think we've got 'em because they've walked through the door, and we forget that the door swings both ways. In fact, it's often easier to leave than it was to arrive. And once they're gone, they're gone for good.

Entrepreneurs need to work hard to make sure that the operational system works better than the sales system, to make sure they can keep the promises they make. When you provide customers with good service, you will retain them and make more money from them either because of recurring business, by selling them additional products, or by the referrals they make, bringing in new clients. Word of mouth is still the most powerful form of marketing and you can control what words those mouths say.

Customer expectations can change drastically in a very short time and it is important to know your customers and understand them before they go to look at your competition. Follow your existing clients and make sure you meet their needs.

If you want to make sure you're on the right track, ask your customers for their opinions. Give them surveys to complete after every invoice or support call. Put a system in place where they can lodge complaints and ensure they know about the process. Manage customer service proactively and when a complaint comes in, deal with it quickly and effectively. Then do everything in your power to make sure that's the last time you hear that particular complaint.

Give a damn, make sure they know that you do and they will too. Grow your customer base, don't just replace it.

---

*If you can get a customer, you've got good marketing. If you can keep a customer, you've got a great business.*

---

# RULE
## 86 YOU WILL HAVE BAD DAYS

I know you think you are Superman and that you should always feel and be amazing, but you aren't Kryptonian – you're human – and you will have off days. It's both inevitable, and OK. You will wake up in the morning and for some or other reason you just won't feel up to it. Or you will go to work and something will happen that just flips the switch. It happens to Every Single Person. I have had many.

What really counts is how you deal with it. As entrepreneurs, we just keep pushing and going even when we know we aren't achieving much. It is then when we need to have the wisdom to do what is right, and it is usually to stop and to take a break. You can shorten your bad days by doing something useful with them.

Go home and have a nap, or go to the nearest book shop and just let your mind switch off. I like going for a walk (or a run). Get out of the office, leave your phone behind and just walk. It might be the fresh air, or it might be the exercise, but whatever it is, you will feel much better after fifteen minutes. Finish that chapter. Watch a movie.

As leaders, we should identify these moments and take responsibility for them. Don't sit in the office in a bad mood and let your employees deal with the blowback. Don't answer emails or solve problems, because you won't do either very well. Just leave, and only go back when you feel better.

Things won't always go as you plan and you need to learn to be OK with it.

---

*What counts is how you deal with the bad days.*

---

# RULE
## 87　SHIPS NOT SEEN

### BY GIL OVED

*Gil is a friend, an inspiration and one of the most successful entrepreneurs in our country. He is the co-founder of The Creative Counsel, which he built from scratch into the biggest agency on the continent, and then sold for a wonderfully well-deserved sum.*

A special word in my life, which is one of the very first words I learned to say, a word that I use most often and a word that I credit, singularly, as the secret to my success is WHY. And if you add another word to this – NOT – the question WHY NOT is even more powerful.

You need to be carving new roads, and the secret to surviving and thriving in today's interconnected world is that you need to forget smart and start being stupid. We live in a world of paradigms and everyone is chasing 'smart' all the time. Our brain is wired and conditioned to try to help us find easy answers as it looks through existing patterns and previous experiences. As a result we don't see things right in front of us. Clear your mind, take off your smart cap, put on your stupid hat, and ask one hundred and one questions.

A scientific term, 'Ships Not Seen', refers to situations when a person has something right in front of them – a concept, a theory, an idea – and even though it is right there within easy reach, they simply cannot perceive it. When the Native

American Indians on the Caribbean islands first saw Christopher Columbus' ship they had no knowledge in their brains that clipper ships existed. And the result? They simply did not see the ships on the horizon. The shaman, however, could see the ripples in the ocean and he wondered what was causing this movement effect in the water. Every day he went to the beach to look at the water, and only after a long period of time was he able to see the shape of what we know were ships. Once the shaman saw them he told everyone in the village that ships exist, and because all the people trusted and believed in him they then saw the ships too. Companies have been destroyed because of 'ships not seen' and dangers to their industries that have been right in front of them, because they simply didn't think outside the box.

It is a brave new world. Every business, regardless of what industry it is in, is a tech company. And every division within the business should see itself as a tech startup. Technology is now how you sell your product, stay connected with your customers, and run a more efficient business.

If you want to succeed in the future world economy you need to change things, you need to do the things that others won't do and you need to see the things that others don't see.

You need to:
- Question everything and remain curious
- Be stupid
- Dream BIG
- Be the master of your destiny and the director of your life
- Be the grandmaster of your game

And remember, always stay humble.

# RULE
## 88

# CONTROL ONLY WHAT YOU CAN

Many years ago I was taught the concept of emptiness. In essence, it is the principle that nothing has any meaning and nothing exists, until you attach meaning to it. It doesn't seem like that in the real world. It seems as though everything exists and has meaning, that everything is coming at us and not from us.

Let's use an example. If there is an irritating person in your life, you assume that that person is irritating to everyone. That the person is simply *irritating*. But somehow that same person has a husband or wife, kids who love them, parents and friends who back them up. You can't stand him or her but they love them. The irritating person is coming from YOU. Actually, an irritating person can't exist without YOUR irritation.

This applies elsewhere. When a taxi driver suddenly stops in front of you, you may ignore it, slow down or put on some Vivaldi, while the person behind you will start swearing, honking their horn, making gestures and generally causing a ruckus. The situation didn't change for the two drivers, just the responses to it. You can't control what happens in front of you, but you can control how you react to the stimulus. And that makes all the difference.

Once you understand this concept and make it part of your life view, you will have the power to change everything. You will have the ultimate power to create your own life and how you feel about everything. 'Bad' things will still happen, but you will deal with them differently. You won't take anything personally and will realise that nothing other people do to you is because of you. It is because of them. You'll see value where you once only saw irritation.

It is much easier said than done, but the results in business will be incredible from day one. You will approach employees, difficult clients and your competition in a completely different way. You will feel in total control, you will have full clarity and you will act accordingly. Plus, you'll have fewer people to annoy you.

Just try it!

---

*You'll see value where you once only saw irritation.*

---

# RULE 89

## THE MYTH OF THE GLASS OCEAN

I often hear people ask when 'things will get easier'. We assume that when we've ironed out all the issues, things will be easy from that point onwards. If you can ever get to this point, and things are truly 'easy' after that, I'd like to write my next book with you. We'll make a fortune. While the problems may be finite, the number of them is not. There is no end. Things will always be rocky. There will always be another hurdle to leap, or a pothole to patch. The ocean will always have waves, and that will never change.

If you ever get to the point of selling your business, that will be your end. You will hand over ownership of it and you will walk right out the door and onto the golf course.

There is no destination in entrepreneurship; it is a continuous journey for as long as you do it. Challenges will always remain. They may be constantly changing, but they will always be there. You'll start out needing to raise money, then you'll need to get clients and then to scale up. Once you scale, you will find it even more challenging to run a bigger business and you will have more compliance issues to deal with.

You need to embrace challenges and see them as part of business and as normal as breathing. Once you make this mind-shift, business will become easier and dealing with challenges will be part of your everyday hustle. Keep your eyes on where you are, not searching for some mythical, utopian future.

Work towards that destination but know that it will forever be changing. Chase it, but enjoy the ride and you will soon find out that there is no destination, no end point. The journey is it.

*The ocean will always have waves.*

# RULE
## 90

# IT ALL REALLY DEPENDS ON YOU

People often ask me for advice – how to get there, my biggest lesson, my tips, my tricks.

We make 'getting there' – wherever 'there' might be – into such a big secret, as if only a few know this and we are constantly looking for the answer, the magic trick. But is there really one? Or is the answer one that we actually don't want to hear?

In my opinion, and in my experience, and in my life, and in my own journey, it is so damn simple. You are the result of the things you do. You reap what you sow. To get what you want, you must decide where you want to be and hustle your butt off to get there because nobody else is going to do it for you.

Look at your own life right now. Whatever you have produced – like it or not – all came from YOU. You are 100 per cent the result of whatever you have or don't have. You are the result of your choices, your actions, your thoughts, your experiences. It is so damn simple, yet we refuse to accept it. Why? Because it is too hard to acknowledge that we are the architects of the average, lukewarm lives we created.

We look at outside factors, we blame the world, we blame our families, our bosses, our past, we blame Brexit, the government, the economy. I believe it is a natural reaction for us to come up with an excuse instead of stepping up and taking responsibility. We live in a world filled with excuses and, sadly, we have subconsciously accepted it.

But let's take a step back and take an honest look at our own lives.

How much time do you spend every day working on YOU? How much time do you spend every day working on your dream? In the last 90 days, how many books have you read? What did you eat? How hard did you train? What kind of investment have you made in YOU? Isn't that a reflection of who you are today? I bet it is!

I've always said that if you wake up at 05h00 every day, if you sweat at least once a day and if you put ten hours into whatever you want to achieve and you do this CONSISTENTLY for three years, it is absolutely IMPOSSIBLE not to have what you want.

Success does not require you to look out the window; it only requires that you look in the mirror. The one person you can blame for everything you have or don't have, is looking right back at you. If you are willing to look at that person in the mirror and say 'I'll make a commitment to you from this moment on that, whatever it takes, I'll do it.' It is IMPOSSIBLE that your life will be the same 90 days from now.

I'm here today to tell you that most people say that they want to be successful, but they don't want it badly enough. They just *kinda* want it. They don't want it more than they want to party. They don't want it as much as they want to be on their phones. Most of them don't want success as much as they want to sleep.

You can say that you *want* to be a successful entrepreneur, or whatever else. But you won't be successful until the day that you say 'I want THAT more than I want anything else', and then act on it.

I get so fed up when people don't hustle but expect all the great things the hustlers get. It's for this reason that the finishing line is not crowded and the reason that it's a beautiful place to be.

---

*Most people say that they want to be successful, but they don't want it badly enough.*

---

# FINAL WORDS

When I started writing this book I wondered whether I would ever be able to find so many rules for entrepreneurs. Now that I'm at the end, I have actually had to remove some of the topics. The rules in this book reflect my experiences and opinions; they are what I've witnessed in successful entrepreneurs and in my own journey. Some might disagree with them and some might add many more. The journey of an entrepreneur is unique and each will be different.

If you take up this *ad*venture, you will be forced to grow as an individual like at no other time in your life, but you will sacrifice many things along the way. You will give up security so that you can have ultimate freedom. Things will get tough, things will always change. You will have hard days and you will also have amazing days.

In the end, what will make it all worthwhile? Yes, having a great business, having loads of cash and freedom, making a difference – but this will all mean nothing if you didn't have fun along the way. Regardless of what the journey looks like, make it a mission to see that it is a fun one.

What is the biggest rule for entrepreneurs? Call it RULE 91, if you like, and it's this:

**ENJOY THE JOURNEY, AND HAVE FUN!**

> *It will all mean nothing if you didn't have fun along the way.*

# SOME APPRECIATIONS

A massive shout out to everyone who has supported my journey as an entrepreneur and those who made this book possible.

Tracey McDonald, my publisher, for the opportunity and for bearing with an entrepreneur who had to run businesses while writing. Tom Asker and the team at Little, Brown for taking my dream to the world. Everyone behind the scenes, who took 35,000 words and turned it into a great product. Dave Meyer from Year Zero, one of the smartest and most intelligent guys I know, who turned average into epic – thank you! Thanks to my friends and fellow entrepreneurs who contributed to the book with their own rules. My fellow Sharks: Dawn, Vinny, Romeo, Gil.

Those companies and individuals who have launched a platform for me to share more of what I do: Rapid Blue Productions, Kee-Leen and Duncan, Idea Candy, Wim Steyn, kykNET, M-Net and the media as a whole. Nadine Todd and *Entrepreneur* mag.

My business family: all our clients and employees. Farren, Marlize, Charnette, Mariska, Gid, Martin, Anina, Felix, Jean-Henry, Amy, Rea, Amanda, Nhlanhla, Gerleze, Akhona, Francois. Investec Bank, Flavio, Michael, Jared. Fred Enslin. Ken Kemp. Charles Hattingh.

Thanks to Xero. A company which has always supported me, and which is changing the business world for entrepreneurs